T0285418

Ordinary Mysticism

Ordinary Mysticism

Your Life as Sacred Ground

Mirabai Starr

HARPERONE

An Imprint of HarperCollins*Publishers*

Journal entries and river notes on pages 115–19 printed with permission from Nancy Laupheimer.

The poem on page 163 originally appeared on the blog *A Hundred Falling Veils* on October 2, 2022. © Copyright Rosemerry Wahtola Trommer.

Some of the names and identifying details of people discussed in this book have been changed to protect their privacy.

The QR codes in this book contain links to websites hosted by third parties. HarperCollins Publishers cannot guarantee that they will remain functional following publication of this edition.

HarperCollins books may be purchased for educational, business, or sales promotional use. For information, please email the Special Markets Department at SPsales@harpercollins.com.

FIRST EDITION

Designed by Janet Evans-Scanlon

Library of Congress Cataloging-in-Publication Data has been applied for.

ISBN 978-0-06-331719-2

24 25 26 27 28 LBC 5 4 3 2 1

Each chapter within this book includes a guided meditation.
To listen to a recording of these meditations
read by Mirabai Starr, visit:

https://mirabaistarr.com/ordinary-mysticism-meditations

To Amy Starr and Roy Starr,
who fill my life with holy irreverence

CONTENTS

Ordinary
Mysticism

Introduction

Demystifying Mysticism

Welcome to the temple of your regular life. The garden of your days, the harbor where you catch your breath, the theater of your relationships. This is the terrain where you wake up and transform. The sometimes chaotic, frequently fraught, unexpectedly beautiful domain of the everyday. You do not need to trek to a remote shrine in the Himalayas, enroll in expensive seminars, or convert to a new religion to connect with spirit. Your life is holy ground. And you are a mystic.

I know you are because all it means to be a mystic is to have a direct experience of the sacred. You have had zillions of those. You may be having one right now. Some resonance in your bones that whispers, *Yes, I belong. I am intertwined with all that is.* A mystic is someone who skips over the intermediaries (ordained clergy, prescribed prayers, rigid belief systems) and goes straight to God.

Meaning, someone who experiences the divine as an intimate encounter, rather than an article of faith. A mystical experience may or may not be connected to established spiritual traditions, theological structures, or faith communities. Mysticism is not about concepts; it is about communion with ultimate reality. And ultimate reality is not some faraway prize we claim when we have proved ourselves worthy to perceive it. Ultimate reality blooms at the heart of regular life. It shines through the cracks of our daily struggles and sings from the core of our deepest desires.

A mystic knows beyond ideas, feels deeper than emotions, is fundamentally changed by that which is unchanging. Mysticism is a way of seeing—beyond the turmoil, the rights and wrongs, the good guys and villains—to the radiant heart of things. The mystical gaze reveals the miracle in the summer thunderstorm and the bowl of ramen. It glimpses the face of the holy in the withered dahlias and blesses the sound of the siren in the middle of the night. It quickens the heart with yearning and soothes the soul with the felt presence of the sublime. A mystic gazes through the eyes of love, and love reveals itself as the only true thing.

For most of us, mystical seeing does not happen all the time, but for all of us, it happens some of the time. And for more and more of us, it is happening more and more of the time. In proportion to current challenges of systemic inequity and climate catastrophe, the flowering of grassroots activism and the uncovering of ancestral trauma in our own family systems, old filters are burning away and we are granted renewed access to the numinous nature of reality. When you decide to walk the path of the mystic, the mundane shows up as miraculous, the boring becomes fascinating, and your own shortcomings turn out to be your greatest gifts.

Guess What? The God You Don't Believe In Is the Same God I Don't Believe In.

There is a persistent rumor that mysticism is inextricably tangled up with religion. Let me dispel this. Organized religion can, in fact, be an obstacle to direct experience of the sacred. Most religious institutions insist that you purchase their brand of God and forsake all others. Not only do they demand exclusivity, but they require intermediaries for anyone to even hang out with the divine. Priests and gurus, with their rote prayers and circumscribed rituals. You have to pass through a series of churchy gates to gain access even to God's suburbs. And once you do, there is to be no talk of actual intimacy with the Holy One. The function of most clergy and their customs is to get you to live whatever they deem to be a godly life, not to actually connect with God. Let alone to become one with God.

Maybe God-talk makes you nervous. You equate the word with the suffocating little boxes of your childhood, being forced to go to Sunday school where you learned that God is old, white, male, and constantly pissed off. He floods the whole world when a few of his kids misbehave, smites cities and drowns armies, issues his orders on tablets of stone, making a big deal about the obvious. Of course you shouldn't kill people (unless, of course, you're God) or steal your neighbor's horse or be rude to your mom and dad. It embarrasses you to even be included in the same breath as those nutty fundamentalists who take every word of the Bible literally and condemn queer people to hell. A true believer you are not.

And yet.

There is a stirring in your soul not because of but rather in spite of religiosity. You sense the presence of something vast and loving when you reach the summit of a mountain or stand up on your surfboard or cup your hand to drink water from a stream. You recoil from the notion that a supreme being is keeping track of your lustful thoughts and yet cannot be bothered to prevent genocide or reverse climate change. If that's what God is, you want no part of it. More atrocities have been committed in the name of God than you can bear to ponder. You have no use for a magical puppet master with a grudge.

Guess what? The god you don't believe in is the god I don't believe in.

My God is sometimes Goddess. She is often subversive, knocking over the furniture in the parlors of the privileged. My God rarely conforms to a fixed gender, embodying all the most life-giving qualities of both the feminine and the masculine, such as tenderness and mystery, discipline and confidence. My God both transcends anything I could conceive of and lives inside of everything I know and do and am.

Even religion.

God sometimes can be found in the temple and the mosque, the chapel and the ashram. For example, singing the ancient Hebrew prayers on Yom Kippur, pleading with the Holy One to bring your wandering heart back home, can be a powerful catalyst for a mystical experience. Or holding out your hand to receive the blessed sacrament and looking up to see the face of the priest gazing at you with kindness. Or silently uttering the name of Allah on each of your ninety-nine prayer beads, and then starting again, and again, until Allah is carried on your breath. Or lighting a stick of incense and waving it in front of a statue of Hanuman, the monkey god, who orchestrated the rescue of the goddess Sita from the clutches of the ten-headed demon and cleared the way for her return to her beloved Ram, reconciling the sundered masculine and feminine faces of the godhead and restoring balance to the universe. Reading the poetry of Lao Tzu can open a mystical state of consciousness: *The Tao that can be told is not the eternal Tao; the name that can be named is not the eternal name.* Or the Gnostic verse: *Cleave a piece of wood, I am there; lift up the stone and you will find me there.* Or a gospel song: *There is a balm in Gilead.*

The trick is to recognize anything that dares to stand in for the Real Thing and let it go—anyone who claims that they alone hold the key to Truth, any community that compels conformity and denounces the Other. Mystical experience is an intimate connection with Love Itself. Mystics have no patience with proofs for the existence of God. They want only to find the holy ripening inside the berry patch, flaming forth from a broken marriage and depleted bank account, permeating the dry land of an aging body, and quieting a troubled mind in the darkest hours of the night.

My friend James Finley—a living mystic if ever there was one—puts it like this: "If we are absolutely grounded in the absolute love of God that protects us from nothing even as it sustains us in all things, then we can face all things with courage and tenderness and touch the hurting places in others and in ourselves with love."[1]

---

1 James Finley, *Intimacy: The Divine Ambush,* CD and MP3 (Center for Action and Contemplation, 2013).

Burning My Robes

After decades on a spiritual path, I have found myself growing increasingly allergic to the codified beliefs espoused by organized religion. At the same time, my thirst for the sacred is deeper than ever. There is no aspect of my life now that is not about finding and sustaining a direct connection with the divine. This is not as serious as it sounds. The more I shed the trappings of faith, the brighter the light grows, and the greater my capacity for childlike wonder and spontaneous delight. A wild creativity has seeped into my responsibilities, infusing the most ordinary moments with magic. I am irreverently reverent now, and do not hesitate to make fun of that which once intimidated me—religious rules, the vocabularies and dress codes of spiritual communities, the checklists that imply there is some perfect order we must strive for. I am way more inclined to laugh at myself now.

To be fair, religious skepticism was baked into the cake of my upbringing. My parents were both raised in secular Jewish families that were far more interested in contributing to social change than in worshipping an invisible deity. They noted that most of the atrocities in the world have been committed in the name of religion. My mom and dad did not limit their critiques to the Judeo-Christian faiths. They were quick to uproot the hypocrisy in the alternative paths that many members of our counterculture community adopted—Buddhist meditation and Hindu devotion, Sufi practices and Native American rituals—to replace the oppressive churches of their childhoods. Patriarchy nestled in the hierarchy, like a snake among wildflowers. Elitism disguised as enlightenment.

This did not stop me from rushing into the arms of almost every spiritual tradition I encountered. During my early teens, I began meditating and practicing yoga. I cultivated my lifelong devotion to a guru from India, explored the ecstasy at the heart of Islam, read the aphorisms of Dogen and the Sermon on the Mount, and reclaimed the ancient wisdom at the core of my own Jewish heritage. Later, through multiple twists of fate, I became a translator of the Spanish mystics and wove Christian mysticism into the tapestry of my interfaith soul. Although I was never drawn to fundamentalism in any form, I was irresistibly attracted to any spiritual teachings that promised an experience of transcendence.

Hoping to tie my camel as close as possible to the wellspring of the human spirit, I became a scholar of world religions and a professor of philosophy and religious studies. Outside the classroom, I continued to find belonging in multiple spiritual spaces: Hindu ashrams and Buddhist centers, Sufi dancing and women's circles. The world's wisdom ways have never stopped guiding and sustaining me, but I no longer endow them with any more power than the potential of a rainstorm to reveal the deepest secrets of the universe.

A friend of mine who is an ordained Zen priest and has dedicated thousands of hours to contemplative practice admits with a sly smile that he has always known he would one day "burn his robes." That day has not yet come, but he is not afraid of it. That's how it is for me. The vestments I have acquired no longer interest me. It's not so much that I have the urge to light them on fire. They are just slipping off, dropping to the floor. I'm stepping out of them and walking away.

Seeded

Ordinary Mysticism is the ripened fruit of a lifetime of study, practice, and teaching across and beyond the world's great wisdom traditions. Every one of my books has been someone else's idea, including this one. Which fits my personality: I'm not someone who is going to crash the party; I need to be invited. My translations of the Spanish mystics came from a conversation with a colleague in which I was kvetching that my students taking introductory philosophy and religious studies courses were finding the existing translations stuffy and dense, and he encouraged me to create a fresh version of my own. A natural outflow of translating the mystics was to write *about* them, which is what I was asked to do next. Then came the call to do a book about the common heart of the Abrahamic faiths. After that, I was persuaded to focus on the women mystics across all the spiritual traditions. *Ordinary Mysticism* was born out of a conversation with my friend Anne Lamott, who calls the process of beholding how the divine overflows the banks of everyday life "Mysticism 101."

Each chapter of this book invites you to reclaim the inherent sanctity of a different aspect of the human condition, as made manifest in unique and intricate you: from setting your intention to walk a mystical path to cultivating your capacity to perceive everything as sacred; to learning from the wise ones who have come before us and recognizing your own innate wisdom; to building and tending community and harvesting the sweet fruits that ripen in the dark nights of your soul; to relinquishing the notion that enlightenment is a one-shot deal and daring to live as a lighthouse of love in this stormy world. Through stories of the mystics of various spiritual traditions, anecdotes from my own life, and accounts of ordinary extraordinary people I know, I offer glimpses of what it could look like to claim your life as holy ground. At the end of each chapter, I suggest a practice to help you orient toward that sacred something I believe your soul really wants, and a writing prompt to explore the secrets your soul is dying to reveal. Truths that, when you uncover them, lift up the whole world.

My Prayer for You

My prayer for you is that you will fearlessly look upon your life as holy and whole. That you will find meaning and wonder bubbling from the ground of your most ordinary moments—applying for a job as a barista or attending a parent-teacher conference, dating again after the end of a long marriage or pulling weeds in your urban garden. Maybe you attend Sunday services at a cathedral, or you prefer to praise the divine in the temple of nature. Perhaps you believe that Christ is the Son of God and Mary is God's mom, or you dismiss all religious beliefs as artifacts of magical thinking. Agnostic or true believer, scientist or hospital chaplain, retired or building a career, this book is for you. It is a little bell to bring you back to yourself and remember how luminous you are—how connected and noble and miraculous.

Here's my prediction: As we propagate the world with wild mystics, the citadels of hate will naturally crumble and fall. Beauty will cascade from every crevice, and we will all find each other irresistible—even those we once would have canceled. We will see ourselves reflected in the still waters and we will like what we see. We will gather wisdom wherever we walk and share it with extravagant generosity.

Practice

MINDFUL MIND, HEARTFUL HEART

Mindfulness practice, rooted in ancient Buddhist philosophy and adapted to meet the psychological realities of our times, has had a meaningful impact across society, independent of spiritual belief systems. But in some ways the movement has stalled out with the head. In this guided meditation, we reclaim the loving heart behind the quiet mind.

Please begin by taking three full breaths. Inhale deeply; exhale completely. Linger in the space between the inhalation and the exhalation. Become curious about the full arc of each breath. Feel the way that breathing with intention fills your body with well-being, revitalizing and calming at the same time.

Now think of a personal situation that is troubling your heart, perhaps an argument with a friend, or the loss of a loved one. It could simply be disappointment about the outcome of a project at work, or a sense that you keep picking different versions of the same unavailable partner and can't seem to figure out why. Maybe the hurt is fresh and hot, or maybe it's something that happened long ago, but in this moment, you can easily connect with the ache of longing, the sting of betrayal, the wish for things to be other than they are.

Stay right here. Gently open yourself to the pain. Unclench your fist. Soften. If someone you were close to has died, offer that being your complete attention. You are showing up for your grief not as a grim spiritual exercise designed to prove how spiritual you are. Rather, you are turning toward what is—in this case, a shattering loss—as an act of love. Love for the person you miss. Love for reality itself.

Allow this tenderness to spread like melted butter through your whole heart and seep into your bones. Let it pool in your belly and illumine your cells. Be willing to cultivate the fullness of your attention as an offering to your loved one. Welcome your particular version of the human condition with curiosity and kindness, taking your rightful place in an infinite network of mutual belonging. Praise this. Forgive reality. Love reality.

Sit in stillness for a few moments, and when you are ready, fold your hands over your heart, utter a silent wish for the well-being of all, and go about the rest of your day.

⚤

WRITING PROMPT

For the prompts at the end of each chapter, I invite you to approach writing as spiritual practice, as prayer, as a portal through which the sacred may come flowing, transfiguring your mind and heart in surprising ways. Expect the unexpected. Welcome the edgy, the irreverent, the undomesticated you.

I recommend you set a timer for ten minutes and then blast off, writing without stopping, outrunning your judgy mind by keeping your hand moving. Let whatever arises spill onto the page. You can use pen and paper or an electronic device. Write in a quiet, private place or a busy coffee shop, out in nature or at the kitchen table.

For the duration of this practice, banish your internal censor, that critical voice that is forever trying to bully you into obeying rules that make no soul-sense. Stay grounded in your body. Avoid abstract concepts and philosophical jargon in favor of specific sensory details. Transmute the lead of mental musings into the gold of living language.

When you are finished, share what you wrote with someone you trust. Ask them not to analyze, critique, or praise it, but rather to simply bear witness. Consider leading a small group practice using the prompt and then reading to each other without commentary, offering and receiving the gift of complete attention.

I find the presence of the sacred hidden in . . .

ONE

Intention

Deciding to Be the Mystic You Already Are

Your Messy Little Temple

I think you get it: You don't have to enter a monastery to be a mystic. You don't have to renounce chocolate or forsake pop culture. It is not necessary to take formal vows and beat yourself up when you inevitably fail to uphold them. These are static notions of what it means to be committed to the life of the soul, and they probably have almost nothing to do with the warm and spicy sprawl of your days. To be a mystic in our times is not about renunciation; it is about intention.

Living as a mystic means orienting the whole of yourself toward the sacred. It's a matter of purposely looking through the lens of love. Contemporary wise woman Anne Lamott says (quoting

Father Ed, the priest who helped Bill Wilson start up Alcoholics Anonymous) that "sometimes Heaven is a new pair of glasses." You know what it looks like when you wipe a lens clean of smears and dust. And you also know how it feels to bump into the furniture when your vision is fuzzy. When you say yes to cultivating a mystical gaze, the ordinary world becomes more luminous, imbued with flashes of beauty and moments of meaning. The universe responds to your willingness to behold the holy by revealing almost everything as holy. A plate of rice and beans, the Dow Jones Industrial Average, your new baby, the latest political scoundrel, the scary diagnosis, the restless nights.

You can start right here, in the middle of your messy life. Your beautiful, imperfect, perfect life. There is no other time, and the exact place you find yourself is the best place to enter. Despite what they might have taught you at Bible Camp or in yoga class, you are probably not on your way to some immaculate state in which you will eventually be calm and kindly enough to be worthy of a direct encounter with the divine. Set your intention to uncover the jewels buried in the heart of what already is. Choose to see the face of God in the face of the bus driver and the moody teenager, in peeling a tangerine or feeding the cat. Decide. Mean it. Open your heart, and then do everything you can to keep it open. Light every candle in the room.

I have an eclectic collection of "candles"—little lights that guide me back home to myself. I kindle them, they burn down or a stray breeze blows them out, I replace them and light them again. Sometimes I blow them out on purpose to take a break from luminosity.

My candles include spiritual superstars like Mother Mary and the Dalai Lama, and unknown sages like the woman who sells newspapers at the intersection and delivers messages from the dead, and her autistic daughter who repeats my name over and over in a loud whisper so that she can get it right: *MIR-A-BAI.* Sacred scriptures from all the world's religions are candles for me: the Hebrew psalms, which cultivate my holy awe; the Beatitudes, which reassure me that my gentleness is strength; the *Tao Te Ching*, which reminds me to behave like water and flow around perceived obstacles; the Upanishads, which dare to suggest that I am that which I seek; the hadith of the Prophet Muhammad, which, contrary to what popular media in the West leads us to suppose, declare that paradise lies at the feet of women; and the Buddha's Deer Park sermon, which describes the sweet spot between overindulgence and artificial austerity. Every kind of music can be a candle for me: chanting the divine names in Sanskrit and Hebrew or listening to Middle Eastern women hip hop artists and Mozart's Requiem, singing folk ballads in the bathtub or playing Lou Reed on my Bluetooth speaker as I chop vegetables for dinner. Political engagement is a candle, languid sex on a Saturday afternoon is a candle, climbing a mountain and feeling my legs and lungs heat up and grow strong or sitting very still with my back against a redwood tree are all candles I light.

When we make a pact with ourselves to show up for reality just as it is, reality rewards us by revealing its hidden holiness, its ordinary wonder, its fruitful shadows and radiant wounds. Not always, not everywhere, but more and more often and in the places we least expect. Setting the intention to walk the way of love rescues us from the all-consuming preoccupation with what modern chant master Krishna Das calls "the movie of Me" in which we endlessly star, casting ourselves as both hero and villain, keeping up an endless flow of critical reviews.[1] Claiming the plot of our regular lives as sacred ground can dispel the clouds of self-absorption and calm the monkey mind that bounces from banana to banana, and steady our twitchy nerves. It takes effort to find the gold in what you once discounted: your own aging skin and ethnic nose, the grouchy grocery store clerk and the slow driver on the one-lane road, a stomach flu on your first day off in ages. But it gets easier. Your wonder-muscles grow more robust and your capacity for appreciation expands.

Wait! What Just Happened?

It is likely that you have not reached this stretch of your road unscathed. Tragic things have happened to you. And aggravating things, and scary things. Perhaps the travesty of an abusive childhood has finally started sinking in, or you find yourself making the same bad choices you have been making for decades. If you have suffered a recent loss, you are likely reeling right now, gasping for breath. It could be that the world itself, with its vast array of political and environmental catastrophes, leaves you feeling panicky and exhausted. Dare to believe that when firestorms ravage the landscape of your life, you are standing on holy ground.

---

1 Krishna Das, "Movie of Me, Now Playing 24 Hours a Day," Awakin.org, https://www.awakin.org/v2/read/view.php?tid=2452.

I know it doesn't feel like that. Holy? It feels charred and askew. You are compelled to rush forth and clean up the mess, fix what is broken, and get on with your regular life. It's not your fault that holiness is not the first or even second thing you perceive amid the wreckage of whatever terrible thing happened to you. Society has conditioned us all to fight impermanence, to resent reality, to wrest control from the clutches of crisis as quickly as possible, with minimal damage to our preconceived notions about how life is supposed to be.

Maybe your sister died last year. Your sister was the only person left in your life who shared your childhood memories—the sweet ones and the dark ones. She is the one you called when someone you loved died. Only now, you can't call her because it *is* her. That feels all wrong, as if the helicopter of your life hit a power line and sent you spiraling into the alfalfa field far below. Who are you if you are not your sister's sister?

Maybe your boss used the COVID pandemic as an excuse to hand over your job to someone with a fancy new teaching certificate, and suddenly, all those times your classroom became a flash point of revelation for a previously apathetic kid, all the money you spent on your own education, all the hours at the kitchen table marking student essays when you would have much rather been skiing, feel like a complete waste. Who are you if you are not quoting Shakespeare to sixteen-year-olds?

Maybe your younger husband fell in love with his even younger yoga teacher. You can't stop imagining the way he looks at her, lustfully and worshipfully, the way you always wished he would have gazed at you but never did. Instead, he treated you a bit like his mother—affectionate, annoyed, indulgent. As if he always loved you *anyway*. Despite all the reasons not to. After all, his eyes told you, nobody is perfect. Except, apparently, the yoga teacher. Who are you if you are not desired?

Maybe a routine mammogram revealed a lump you never detected while circling your breast in the shower with soapy hands. Weeks go by before they can schedule a lumpectomy, during which your mind serves up a never-ending stream of dire scenarios and you carry your anxiety like a bucket of gasoline everywhere you go and splash it on everyone who comes into proximity. Wait! You are not finished with your life! You have a book to write, you never learned to play the piano your Aunt Mary left you, and your grown children still think you damaged them beyond repair. Who are you if you are not a perfect specimen of a human being?

I invite you right now to stand in the fire of your angst, to take your seat in free fall, to let yourself down into the arms of the void. To stop where you are and take a breath, and then another, and a third. Allow your brain chemistry to do its thing, while you take stock of the present moment. See whether you can cultivate an iota of curiosity about the shape and fragrance and contours of what *is*—your beautiful broken heart, your shattered dreams, your weariness. Allow a measure of tenderness to seep through the torn seams and soothe you. Notice a luminescence just behind the dense blackness, like the moon softening the edges of a snowy night.

This is what it means to be a mystic. To show up for what is, to be present to all that is, to take refuge in the boundless intimacy of exactly what is. The love your heart yearns for flows from the hidden spring that lies directly under your feet, precisely on your own most ravaged patch of earth.

Subversive Sages

The historic saints, mystic poets, and peacemakers we admire most were a bunch of renegades. They operated within the frameworks of their religious traditions and yet broke the rules and opened the way for others to have their own experience of the sacred states they described. Generally, the community recognizes its sages before institutions do. In many cases the religious and political leaders do not know what else to do with these holy troublemakers, and so eventually they end up canonizing them.

Take Francis and Clare of Assisi. They were both born into privileged families in medieval Italy. Francis's father was a prosperous cloth merchant who expected his son to join the family business. Clare was born into the noble class, a dwindling population desperately clinging to its power. When Francis abdicated his wealth to live among the poorest of the poor, he was subverting not only the prevailing values of his family, but of his culture. Clare too. She ran away from home to join Francis in building a movement dedicated to voluntary simplicity and kinship with the natural world. They suffered for their efforts—speaking truth to power inevitably pisses off the authorities—but they also blossomed, propagating a garden of joyful praise that still reverberates eight centuries later.

Francis's life, his death, and the love he shared with Clare are woven into the tapestry of legend. "Praise to you, our sister Mother Earth!" Francis sang from his deathbed in the courtyard of Clare's cloistered convent. This version poetically proclaims that it was in the agony of his dying that he composed one of the most glorious prayers in the history of religious literature, the Canticle of the Creatures. And that when he died, the brothers lifted his body to Clare's window so that she could touch him before they carried him away. Francis and Clare may not have had sex, but they were lovers. Lovers of each other, lovers of the poor, lovers of the whole of creation.

I can think of a dozen women mystics who declined marriage in favor of a life dedicated to prayer and contemplation. Even if religion turns you off, you have to admire their verve. Most of these women were breaking out of upper-class cages. Often they were facing marriages with men much older than themselves that had been arranged by other people for the purpose of political alliance. Love was out of the question. What mattered was perpetuating the systems and structures that kept the rich rich and the poor poor.

My namesake, the sixteenth-century devotional poet from India, known simply as Mirabai or Meera, is a great example of a woman who defied the existing expectations of her community and ran off with Krishna, the Lord of Love. Well, not in physical form, but Mirabai's heart belonged to her metaphysical beloved, and she was simply incapable of going through the motions of marriage to a regular human. Problem was, she was engaged at age twelve and wed at sixteen to a petty prince twice her age. Did his family nod their heads understandingly and fold their hands prayerfully in response to Mirabai's passion for God? They did not. Such arrangements were the cement that kept existing societal frameworks in place. Mirabai was rattling the architecture.

And so, as Indian lore tells it, they tried to kill her. First, with a cobra concealed in a garland of flowers placed around the bride's neck. The venomous snake slipped away. Next, with a cup of sweet fruit nectar laced with deadly nightshade, but the toxin was transmuted as soon as it passed through the gate of Mira's lips. Then, with a carpet of rose petals covering a bed of poisoned nails. Mira slept in peace and woke refreshed. When the prince was killed in battle fighting the Moghuls, his family insisted that his wife accompany his body on the funeral pyre, as was the custom. But because Mirabai considered herself married to Krishna and not Bohj Raj, she saw no reason to end her life. She refused to be burned alive. Finally, they gave up and banished her. Perfect! Mirabai spent the rest of her life wandering barefoot throughout northern India, spontaneously uttering poetry and ecstatically dancing for God. She mingled with people of all castes and worshipped with people of multiple religions. The most beloved devotional poet of South Asia, her songs are still sung today. Mira managed to be simultaneously subversive and reverential.

Where Mirabai was born into wealth and privilege, Rabia Basri, a Sufi mystic born in Iraq around 716 CE, was orphaned at a young age and then abducted and sold into slavery. She worked her ass off all day and prayed through the night. According to a story passed down through the ages, one evening, Rabia's master saw a glow emanating from the roof of his compound. He climbed the ladder to see if the house was burning, and there was Rabia, bowing at the feet of the

Invisible, crying out to God—"Allah! Allah!" Flames were leaping from the crown of her head. Convinced that he was in the presence of a saint, the master slipped back down the ladder and in the morning offered Rabia her freedom.

Rabia could have been revered, served, and lavishly supported in the guru game. She received multiple marriage proposals but refused them all. She spent the rest of her life alone in the desert, embracing a path of radical simplicity. Her prayers became poems, and her teachings are widely considered to be the wisest and most robust in the history of Islamic mysticism. Rabia wanted nothing less than everything. That is, unbroken devotion to God alone.

Do you have to pray as if your hair were on fire to qualify as a mystic? You do not. Do you even have to believe in God? I think we have established that the answer is no. Must you leave your suburban life and corporate job, cancel your gym membership and streaming television subscriptions? Is it more spiritual to write mystical poetry than to clean your infant's spit-up off the shoulder of your favorite sweater? No, no! You can be spiritually subversive without being an extremist. You can drink Prosecco and still be spiritual. You can be in love with your favorite human and not disappoint the God of Love. Sleeping in on the weekends does not break your vow to dedicate yourself to the liberation of all beings. It just means you are tired of holding up the world and are taking a minute to recharge.

Our ideas of what it means to be spiritual prevent us from living an engaged spiritual life. It would be a travesty to recruit the mystics and masters we admire from the past to stuff us into cages of piety and shame. Especially when they themselves were wildly free, gloriously rebellious, gleefully countercultural. Be a mystical troublemaker. I dare you.

Makeshift Cathedral

Don't let the patriarchy have all the fun. You have the right to create sacred spaces and populate them with whatever feels holy to you, whatever inspires you, centers you, uplifts you. And it can be ever-changing. Maybe you create a little ancestor altar on your bedroom dresser. You spread a white lace doily your mother's mother tatted, and atop that a picture of that very grandmother when she was nineteen, posing beside her fiancé's car on their way to a dance. Next to Grandma, your favorite photo of your favorite dog who died last year, and behind that a statue of a brown-skinned angel with folded hands. Mix up your spiritual traditions: a statue of Buddha in meditation, your aunt's rosary, a copy of the psalms, and a poem by a Persian mystic. The items of your altar may not be religious at all. Maybe your shrine consists purely of objects from nature—pinecones and geodes, feathers and bones. Drawing on the ancient wisdom of the ancestors, you might include the four elements: a jar of river water, a bowl of dirt, a candle, a flute.

You could start with one array of sacred objects and then take it all down and start again next month. There are no rules. Photographs of saints from India, *New Yorker* cartoons, birthday cards, and erotic art. As an ordinary mystic, you are sanctioned to build temples and enter them, even if your temple is simply an ever-rotating cluster of objects that make you feel like you can breathe again when the world has left you breathless.

When my first boyfriend died in an accident, I turned my bedroom into a shrine. It was the spring I turned fourteen, and a mash-up of normal developmental turmoil plus a predilection for meaning-making had already drenched my world with a poetic intensity.

This was the era of the back-to-the-land movement, and my overeducated Jewish parents had joined the exodus from Middle America to settle in the wild places that capitalism had left behind. The suburban Long Island of my early childhood was a mere memory; we were proud citizens of Hippie Land in New Mexico. My parents had adopted a lifestyle that they called "voluntary simplicity" but that their children experienced as involuntary poverty. My bed was a loft built of peeled ponderosa saplings propped over the water heater in the utility closet. I tacked a tie-dyed sheet along the length of my bunk, and underneath I set up a couple of bricks with a scrap of two-by-four that I covered with a remnant of velvet jacquard I found at the local free box outside Amigos Food Co-op. A woven cotton rug from Mexico, a candle in a glass, a picture of Krishna playing his bamboo flute torn from an expired Indian calendar, and voilà!—an altar.

One morning before school, I climbed down the makeshift ladder, parted the curtain, folded my legs into a half-lotus, lit a stick of incense, and sank into my customary angst—that aforementioned concoction of adolescent biochemistry activated by grief over my boyfriend's recent death. But the play of beauty and shadow, of jasmine and silence, began to soften the edges of my pain, and something like happiness leaked in. It wasn't joy, nor bliss, nor even a newfound optimism. It was simpler than that, less cathartic, and did not jeopardize my attachment to my tragic storyline. It was a kind of soul-satisfaction, both vibrant and soothing. For a moment nothing was missing, and I could let out a breath I hadn't even realized I was holding.

Ever since, I have made every space a sacred space. With a few reliable elements—religious art from various traditions; photographs of the Indian saint Anandamayi Ma, her eyes closed and head tilted in rapture; a porcelain statue of Kuan Yin, goddess of compassion; a woven prayer shawl in shades of green and gold; a tea light nestled in a clay cup; and a package of nag champa incense—I can transfigure any nook into a temple. A corporate hotel room, a forest clearing, a stage where I am leading a workshop, the deathbed of a beloved. My house is a chapel, with little shrines in every room. Tibetan *thangkas* in the stairway, photos of Neem Karoli Baba draped in strings of prayer beads above the stove and beside my desk and on my nightstand, *ofrendas* to my deceased daughter Jenny, sculptures of Our Lady of Guadalupe in every size and style from earthy to refined.

"It feels so good in here," visitors invariably remark. "Like church, but not churchy."

Sometimes people politely inquire whether I get tired of living amid all this religious iconography. I have flirted with a more secular décor, but it makes me feel as if I had been exiled to Kansas, or like I was walking around in someone else's high heels. And besides, I do have nonreligious art—I do! I have abstract pieces by acclaimed painters and also paintings of our otherworldly New Mexico landscape. I have raku pots, Pima baskets, and Zapotec weavings. I have framed photographs of my hippie parents standing on our dilapidated porch in 1973 and a Vietnamese woman selling limes in a busy marketplace. To me, all good art is sacred art, just as all good poetry is mystical poetry (more about that coming up). Beauty blesses everything it touches.

Maybe it's my heritage of wandering Jews who, exiled from the Holy Land by one empire after another, were compelled to replace the great temple in Jerusalem with homespun versions wherever they found themselves in the diaspora. All I know is that long ago I stumbled upon a way to render the broken world a little more whole. Or bigger, somehow, with an increased capacity to hold the brokenness. And at the same time, a little smaller and more intimate, a bit quieter and cozier, a nestling place, a place of refuge, a sanctuary.

Inventing Rituals

On the ridge above the house where my husband, Jeff, and I live is a shrine in the form of a mound of quartz crystals that people have gathered from the floor of the surrounding desert. We are not sure who started it and when or for what purpose, but over the past twenty years or so that we have been hiking up that mountain, it has become a sacred place, a pilgrimage destination. Once or twice a week, in all kinds of weather, from scorching summer sun through the deep snow of winter, Jeff and I trek to the white rock shrine and place a stone for someone who has died. It might be for loved ones long gone, like our dads or our daughter. It is often for someone who has recently left this world, even if we did not personally know them. I always add a prayer for the ones they have left behind. The grieving ones. I especially bless them.

Recently, Jeff introduced me to a place he goes on his solitary walks. At the end of one particular trail is a large slab of granite, shaped like a heart, embedded in the sandy soil. He calls it the Prayer Rock. Jeff circles the rock three times, the way practitioners of Tibetan Buddhism circumambulate a stupa, those domed temple structures believed to be especially potent places for meditation. As he walks in slow circles, he silently chants a mantra. If you knew Jeff, this might surprise you as much as it surprised me. Although he spent his twenties and thirties living in ashrams, Jeff has long since abandoned religious forms of any kind, and his good-natured impiety has given me the courage to stop taking my own spiritual principles so seriously. This makes me trust him even more when he shares something like his Prayer Rock with me. His connection to this spot as a sacred space is spontaneous, organic, and authentic.

I have been to many religious gatherings where the worshippers mixed up the doorway for the room—that is, they were so caught up in the details of the entrance to faith that they seemed to have forgotten that the purpose of a threshold is to step across and go inside. I remember my first time in India, staying at an ashram in the foothills of the Himalayas. The temple zone was actually a large open-air courtyard paved with marble, encircled by shrines to many different deities. Everyone who entered would leave their shoes under a bench outside the temple. The thing is, I was staying inside the ashram, on the other side of the compound, and one day I forgot to remove my shoes and entered the main area with my flip-flops on. I realized my mistake halfway across and decided to make a run for it, dashing to the other side before any harm was done. Too late. A Western woman who had spent years at the ashram raced across the stone floor and reprimanded me in a hushed fury. Her admonishment felt like a slap. My face burned and I yanked the sandals from my feet and carried them the rest of the way to the inner gate. *I did it wrong. I must be wrong. Bad and wrong and beyond redemption.*

Another time, I was at an American ashram where they were conducting a fire puja to commemorate the installation of a new shrine to the divine mother. I had had melanoma surgery a week before, and there was a wound between my shoulder blades where they had removed the malignant mole along with a large margin of surrounding flesh. I probably should not have been out and about so soon after surgery, but the shrine was my friend Nina's project and I wanted to support her. I sat in a second tier of people gathered around the sacred fire circle, chanting mantras and tossing flower petals into the flames after each phrase, my back burning with every gesture, but my soul nourished by the felt presence of the divine feminine. At one point, a young woman sitting in front of me, calling out *"Swaha!"* at the appropriate intervals, swiveled around and gave me a magnanimous smile. She leaned back and whispered that I was not doing it right and, with her slender fingers positioned just so, demonstrated how to properly offer the flowers so that they would not keep falling outside of the sanctioned holy zone. Again, I was flummoxed by the correction. When the next round was complete, I slipped away and went home, thrown off balance by a wave of shame and a corresponding flash of indignation. *I did it wrong. Again.* After all this time of sitting in sacred spaces, I still couldn't get it right.

I have dedicated my adult life to empowering people to connect with their inner wisdom and authority. Their baked-in beauty and goodness. As you can see, in some ways I am full of shit. Because I still feel bad when I accidentally stumble over a religious rule and break it. But friends, I am starting to practice what I preach. I am consciously entering these hallowed spaces—the churches and temples, meditation halls and sweat lodges—with my revolutionary heart leading the way and my sense of humor tucked in my back pocket for easy access. I am inventing rituals for every occasion—whispering prayers beside mountaintop shrines to honor our beloved dead and circumambulating holy rocks to fling blessings in all directions. I officiate weddings in which together we shape the soft clay of the lovers' own words to meet the realities of their love, rather than trying to cram the living thing that is their relationship into a prepackaged box. In my morning meditations I am as likely to read from a collection of political poetry as to contemplate the Bhagavad Gita. I bless all kinds of babies with water I collected outside the Basilica of Our Lady of Guadalupe. I try to welcome the Sabbath every Friday when the sun goes down, as my ancestors did before me, even if I'm at an Italian restaurant in a faraway city, using my phone's flashlight if there are no candles, cranberry juice if there is no wine, pretzels if there is no bread.

You too can create rituals to support and bless any occasion. You can make it holy with the poetry of your wild heart. The most ordinary life experiences become transcendent when you offer them your reverent silence, your mischievous laughter, your sacred rage. Organize the writing of a group poem or the making of a collective work of art as a rite of passage in your family or community. The next time you have sex, light those candles and play that playlist and hold eye contact, as if you were making love with the goddess herself. Believe in your ability to see behind the veil of convention to the luminous center of spirit. I believe in you. I believe in the mystic you are and have always been and ever shall be.

The Myth of the Perfect Family

It's hard to give up our fantasies of a life where beauty is built in and we don't have to work at finding it. It's easy to recognize the presence of the sacred in the saintly hospice chaplain who turns your mother's deathbed into a temple, in an epic sunset over the South Pacific, or in the birth of a baby to a couple who had given up hope of ever conceiving, let alone carrying a child to term. But what about your boring job, your addicted partner, your hometown that feels more like a strip mall than a community? What about your dining room table at dinner time?

One of the things it means to be an ordinary mystic is to bow at the feet of your everyday existence, with its disappointments and dramas, its peaceful mornings and luminous nights, and to honor yourself just as you are. Remember Stephen Stills of Crosby, Stills, and Nash? He told us that if you can't be with the one you love, you should love the one you're with. I say, if you can't be the one you wish you could be, love the one you are. And if you don't have the life you imagined you would or should have by now, how about loving the life you are living? A mystic finds the magic in the midst of the nitty-gritty, the crusty spaghetti sauce pot in the sink and the crocus poking out of a spring snowfall, the unsigned divorce papers on the kitchen table and the results of your latest blood work on your computer screen.

I know that's not always easy. I am continually challenged to stop arguing with reality and instead soften into what is. For instance, my students may think I'm wise, but my kids seem to think I'm a dork. I don't love this disconnect. Like you, maybe, I set myself up with an array of preconceived notions about the kind of family I would like to make, and then beat the shit out of myself when things don't work out the way I envisioned—when my children don't treat me like the March girls treated Marmee in *Little Women*, when I don't behave anything like I thought I would or should as a parent. I made choices that stretched the parenting paradigm to the breaking point before I even began.

For one thing, I married a man who was a quarter of a century older than I was and to whom I had minus-zero sexual attraction. I thought he was interesting (mostly because he told me so) and spiritually evolved (again, self-proclaimed). He also had two children my age and no interest in starting from scratch. But I began to yearn for a baby with biblical fervor, so he agreed to a compromise: we would adopt a school-age child from the foster-care system. This solution appealed to my innate savoir complex, a condition I developed after my older brother died of cancer when he was ten and I became the default eldest child in my family of origin.

I imagined myself selflessly mothering a child with medical challenges, or reanimating a child so broken by abuse that only my love could revive her, an immigrant child from the jungles of Guatemala, maybe, or a child who could not hear or speak. We combed through binders at the special-needs adoption agency. I secretly wished for a quiet five-year-old girl who loved books like I did, but I picked an eight-year-old Black boy with Tourette syndrome. My husband vetoed that choice and set his sights on a ten-year-old girl who had been removed from her South Dakota biker family because of abuse by the most recent of the four fathers of her mother's four children. We drove up to Spearfish from Taos and brought her home.

From the beginning it was clear that I was out of my depth. Dani was exquisite, the child of a Scandinavian mother, an Afro-Caribbean father, and, at eleven, she was already taller and heavier than I was. This wasn't saying much since I am barely five feet tall and don't weigh enough to qualify as a blood donor, but it saddened me that I couldn't easily cuddle her in my lap or give her a bath. She chattered in a steady stream, mostly about TV shows, and she sang country songs about eighteen-wheelers in a high, off-key voice. Also, she lied. Compulsively. Soon after she earned her learner's permit at fifteen, I let her drive to the neighborhood video store on her own, whereupon she promptly drove my car into a ditch while fiddling with the stereo. Where it would have been much easier to tell a straight story about the accident, she concocted an epic tale about being run off the road by a drunk driver, causing me to charge forth in search of the imaginary perpetrator so I could bring him to justice. She regularly confessed to strangers that her new parents kept her locked in the attic except for when we brought her down to perform compulsory labor such as chopping wood and scrubbing floors. Within a year Dani had started her period, filled out into a voluptuous, smoldering beauty who drew a frightening amount of attention from guys much older than herself, and was individuating with all her might.

Two years later, we adopted Jenny. She was four. Jenny's birth mother was an exotic dancer with bipolar disorder, and her biological father was unknown, but obviously Black. The only reason social services agreed to place a child who looked like Jenny with parents like us—I am a freckled Ashkenazi Jew and my former husband was a pasty white guy from Kansas—was because Dani was mixed-race, so we had built-in diversity.

Jenny was an observer. At the beginning, she rarely smiled, and when I hugged her, she grew rigid in my arms. She maintained an aloof and cautious stance for the first few weeks she was with us, and then she surrendered. She was all in, adhering herself to my body, pressing her face against my breasts, preferring to be transported on my hip than to walk, and to be fed from my fingers more than to pick up her own fork. She reverted to baby talk, as if she were making up for the lost years locked in cheap hotel rooms while her other mother turned tricks on East Central Avenue and sometimes forgot to go back for her toddler. And although she didn't like to draw or sing like I did as a child, Jenny had a wildly creative mind that captivated me daily. When she did choose to speak, her vocabulary far surpassed a person of her age, and she strung words together in the most uncommon ways. She had an intense gaze, lips like peony blossoms, and a Zen-like capacity for stillness. Jenny was fiercely devoted to me. Until she wasn't.

Although they were nine years apart, both my daughters were

finished with me by the time they were fourteen and wanted to move out. Which I too had done. I had slipped away from my wonderful mother when she was distracted by saving the world from consumerism, patriarchy, and monogamy. Even as I watched my own daughters pivot, directing all their wrath toward bewildered and infuriated me, I marveled at the way family patterns repeat themselves. It obviously wasn't a genetic blueprint, and yet it carried the aroma of ancestral trauma, nonetheless. The girls in my line come of age, reject their mothers, and cannot wait to leave home. Everything I said was deemed stupid, and all my efforts to create safety were perceived as incarceration. I had left my stifling first marriage soon after Jenny was placed with us, and so I weathered these battles alone, unequipped for the determination with which my children fled from me.

Wasn't I a good person, a good mom? Generous and fun? Sure, I could be moody and explosive; I was not proud of this character defect. Yes, I sometimes chose men over my kids, but these were interludes. I was steadfast in my dedication to parenting. I refused to be a martyr, but I was accountable, and when I fucked up, I made amends. And I was lavishly loving. Whenever I noticed that too much time had gone by without a hug, I would gather my girls in my lap and nuzzle them, cooing silly sentences about how adorable and funny and smart they were. It wasn't enough.

"What they don't tell you when you adopt special-needs kids," I whispered to my friend Lorie, the office manager of the agency through which my children came to me, "is that they are so good at manipulation you can end up acting like a child yourself, all your worst qualities on full display." It felt like sacrilege to admit this.

My carefully constructed persona—radiantly wise and unconditionally loving mother-goddess—dissolved in the fire of reality, and I grieved. Lorie rolled her wheelchair close and pulled me into a quiet embrace while I cried.

Over time, I learned to let go of my fantasy of the perfect family and to find beauty, meaning, and wholeness in the heart of reality. Unpredictable, ever-changing, humiliating, and humbling reality. I began to take a look at the white supremacy embedded in my liberal self-image, noticing the odor of a white savior complex rising from my resentment that my brown children did not appreciate all I had done for them. Eventually, I even came to love unlovable me, against all odds.

Chances are, if you are a parent, whether adoptive or biological, you too have experienced the collapse of your parenting fantasies. You also have received an open invitation to accept the kids you have and forgive the parent you are, with a degree of humility bordering on humiliation and a dash of humor that can sometimes carry maniacal overtones. Whether your children are addicts or activists (or addict-activists), whether they graduated from Stanford or dropped out of high school (or trained as tattoo artists), whether they are working on Wall Street or at McDonald's (or not at all), chances are they have disappointed and worried you at times. The truth? All those families you see on social media that look so happy and healthy have also been strained beyond imagining.

This is the human condition. And at the very center of your own shattered dream, the face of the sacred flashes and glimmers. The holy disaster is a beckoning. Come. Enter the fire of love and let it remake you again and again. To be an ordinary, everyday mystic is to take your rightful place on the throne of what is.

Shattering the Tablets

You may be familiar with this myth. After schlepping all the way up Mount Sinai and staying there until the Holy One had revealed the law and inscribed it on a set of stone tablets, Moses came back down to discover that his people had grown impatient in his absence and reverted to idolatry. They were worshipping the same old golden calf. In a fit of ire, Moses threw down the tablets and they shattered. Back up the mountain he went, returning with a new set carved with his own finger and polished by God.

Let's do a little midrash here. Midrash is the timeless Jewish practice of reflecting on the Torah (the text Christians call the Old Testament). It can get wildly creative, subversive even. That's when new life has a chance of being breathed into stale theology, and outmoded religious messages shape-shift to stay relevant.

Maybe it's not only okay to defy some of the commandments; maybe we're supposed to. Not as a matter of adolescent rebellion but as an act of deep reverence for truth. Take the whole notion of religious injunctions. Thou shalt this and thou hast better not that, or else! Or else what? When you consciously challenge age-old agreements about morality and reality, when you reclaim the rules as invitations rather than threats, you set your soul free to directly experience the divine. A mystical (i.e., direct) encounter.

You've probably already done this, but just in case, I invite you now to deconstruct your inherited version of a punishing Father-

God in favor of an irreverent and hilarious Sister-God who wants you to think for yourself and meet this life with curiosity and glee. Throw those tablets on the ground.

In Judaism, the word *mitzvah* carries layers of meaning. Technically, a mitzvah is a commandment all Jews are required to obey, which is no fair and also not realistic, since there are 613 of them in the compendium of Jewish law. Who could be expected to keep track of things like "a eunuch shall not marry a daughter of Israel" or one should not "eat a worm found in fruit." At a deeper level, a mitzvah is a good deed, such as delivering a Crock-Pot of miso vegetable soup to a friend with COVID or handing out warm socks to unhoused people in the winter. But let's dive all the way in, here. Let's reclaim mitzvah as a blessing.

This one, for example: There is a commonly held belief across the spiritual traditions that we are supposed to give charity anonymously, without any expectation of recognition or compensation. "But when you give to the needy, do not let your left hand know what your right hand is doing, so that your giving may be in secret. And your Father who sees in secret will reward you." So sayeth Rabbi Jesus in the Sermon on the Mount. What sayeth you? Is it so terrible to feel good when you do good? Why is it unspiritual to enjoy the look of gladness on your partner's face when she opens the present you've picked out with care? Your Father in Heaven might advocate for anonymity, but your Mother the Earth rejoices when you rejoice.

In the Bhagavad Gita, one of the most cherished scriptures of Hinduism, Lord Krishna—the God of Love disguised as a humble charioteer—instructs his disciple, Prince Arjuna, to do his duty and dispense with any attachment to outcomes. "Let your concern be with action alone, and never with the fruits of action. Do not let the results of action be your motive, and do not be attached to inaction." Does this mean that when you organize for social change, say, real diversity in the workplace (as opposed to tokenism) or gender-inclusive language in your child's classroom, you're not supposed to care whether or not systemic injustice is dismantled? As your brother-in-law's eyes fill with tears because you bothered to visit him in prison when the rest of your family had given up on him, is it either noble or kind to act like it doesn't matter? "The fruits of your actions are not for your enjoyment," the Gita proclaims. "Even while working, give up the pride of doership." So, I'm supposed to let my hungry heart starve rather than feast on the feeling of wholeness that washes over me when I finish a project, whether reorganizing a closet or composing an opera?

Now, in my opinion, this is not what the authors of the Gita meant at all. But this is the way the Spiritual Boys' Club interpreted it and promulgated it. Organized religion likes to control its followers. We can't have people reveling in delight when they accomplish difficult tasks. It might go to their heads! Puff up their egos, fan the flames of desire. The key to this teaching lies in the subtext: Offer the fruits of your actions to me (the God of Love). Do what you do as an act of prayer. Taking cash from the ATM, picking up your dog's poop from the hiking trail, driving your neighbor to work when her car won't start (again). These are your offerings, and they return to you as blessings. When you extend beyond your own comfort to tend the wounds of the world, the sense of quiet gratification that warms you like a cup of tea on a snowy day is meant for you. It is a gift delivered by the hands of the holy. Open it.

The same is true for vows. In the Christian tradition, a vow is a solemn promise made to God. Often this takes the form of monastic vows, such as when a religious sister vows to obey her superiors (usually men), and a priest vows to remain celibate all his life. A married couple exchanges a vow not to have sex with other people, and the Crusaders vowed to recapture the Holy Land from the Muslims, at any cost. Vows are solemn and uncompromising. They leave little room for the realities of the human condition. Their favorite subject seems to be sex (curtailing it), and next in line is violence (the tragic doctrine of a "just war").

You may not be surprised to hear me question the legitimacy and good sense of this custom. It isn't that I don't believe in setting clear and conscious intentions, such as being faithful to a great love or lightening your footprint on this earth. At our wedding, Jeff and I did not use vow language. We didn't even say "I promise." What we did was list all the things we would do in our marriage, such as "I will share my vulnerability and my power with you" and "I will honor your family as my own." Setting our intentions blesses the outcomes, without investing them with shame or blame if they don't work out. This is what rituals are for. Whether traditional or newly invented, private or communal, religious or secular, ceremonies sanctify life passages, washing new beginnings with a sense of awe and meaning. But intending something with all your heart does not mean you're bound for trouble if you change your mind. It just means that the changes that unfold are sometimes bigger than the containers we built to withstand change.

In Buddhism, the bodhisattva vow is at the center of the Mahayana tradition. This is a promise that, even if you come to the brink of enlightenment, you will not enter until all sentient beings are liberated. This world, says Buddhism, is an ocean of samsara (suffering), and we sometimes feel we are drowning. But the wheel of births, deaths, and rebirths is carrying us toward nirvana (bliss), even if it doesn't always appear that way and even though we get knocked off the path now and then and feel like we are being crushed. So that's comforting: knowing there is an evolutionary trajectory and we are on it. But once you make the bodhisattva vow, you are beholden. You don't get to hop off the wheel and merge with the One. As long as a single blade of grass remains to be liberated, you will stick around to help.

It's a beautiful intention—to stay here in the world of illusion until every last living thing is enlightened—but does it have to be so heavy? How about making of your life a kindhearted offering for the liberation of all beings and the healing of the earth? Not as an injunction but rather as an expression of love, love that percolates from the wellspring of our innate goodness and naturally spills over into the garden of the human condition. Your wish for the well-being of all creation becomes not a prison in which you incarcerate yourself, but a state of lovingkindness in which you take refuge.

Again, I know that this is probably the true meaning of this vow, but the human community does what it does: we turn mystical insight into a reliable set of strictures and then bind ourselves up with them. Untether yourself. The naked essence of a vow is a call to be free.

Thanking Your Life Can Save Your Life

My sister, Amy, would not consider herself to be a mystic. She is weight lifter, a personal trainer, an exercise instructor at a trendy gym who makes a living by guiding people to both embrace their fitness goals and bow to the beauty of their bodies exactly as they are. The mother of two young men she raised by herself (another family pattern, but also a cultural one), Amy is feisty and kind. She knows what she wants, rejects what she doesn't, and gives of herself to her family, friends, and clients beyond all expectation.

Amy has not had great luck with romance. To anyone who knows her, this is bewildering. She is adorable. She is small and curvy, muscular and sensuous. She has a river of golden curls, big blue eyes, and flawless skin. She is funny and smart. She laughs with ease, especially at herself. In partnership she is loyal and playful. And yet Amy has not yet had an enduring relationship.

Most recently, she lived with a young guy who appeared to be utterly devoted. They shared common interests in the fitness world and enjoyed the same quirky elements of pop culture. They moved to a new city where they were both offered great jobs in their industry, and they bought a house together. But before the paint had even dried, the boyfriend was gone. Amy came home from work one afternoon, and he informed her that he didn't want to be with her anymore. By the end of the week all his stuff was gone, and he had moved to an undisclosed location. He did not explain his change of heart, nor did he give Amy the opportunity to ask any questions. He simply vanished, leaving her with nothing but a dreadful sense that she was unlovable.

Even as she plunged into some pretty dark spaces, three things saved Amy, and also broke open the container of her human predicament to reveal the realm of the mystical.

The first was that she let herself plummet. She wept and raged, alternately heaped all the blame on herself to try to prop up the fantasy of his integrity and allowed herself to be lured into the quicksand of self-pity. She felt her feelings and did not turn away. This was a purifying fire. It took many of her cherished illusions to the ground, and when those false structures cleared, the landscape opened. She could see far, and she could see rightly. Amy did not try to rise above her predicament; she descended. She declined to employ any of the many available means for bypassing reality; she walked into the heart of reality. Rather than spiritualizing her experience, she embodied it.

The second thing that saved Amy was gratitude. Even if she had spent all night crying, she rose in the morning, made a cup of gourmet coffee, served it to herself in a beautiful mug, and sat down and made a list of all the things she was grateful for. Some days she couldn't muster more than "my sheepskin slippers" or "the way my boss makes me laugh." Other days she was washed with wonder at the staggering beauty of another sunset in the Sangre de Cristo Mountains and the fact that her mother was still alive when so many of her friends were losing theirs. Each time Amy said yes to the presence of blessings in her life, the blessings multiplied before her eyes. Her heart was broken, and her heart was broken open.

Finally, Amy was sober and realistic about the process. She knew that she would not always be able to maintain a stance of gratitude for the goodness of her life and acceptance of the pain. She allowed herself to hate her circumstances, to refuse to forgive reality for hurting her, to ruminate on how her boyfriend could just leave like that when only days before he had texted her, as he did every day, with little messages of desire and appreciation. There were nights when she wasn't sure living was worth it, and mornings where the very thought of trying to conjure up something to be grateful for made her want to pick up a plate and smash it against the wall of her empty house. She did not fight these moments. She allowed the despair to wash over her. And then she reached out to someone who loved her unconditionally. Like me, her big sister. She let me hold her while she sobbed.

This dance continues. The dance of gratitude and grief, of glimpsing the sublime and naming the disaster, of sinking under the waves and floating in the sunlight. But each time Amy says yes to what is, her equanimity deepens and her capacity for simple joy expands. If being a mystic is about having a direct experience of the sacred nestled in the heart of the ordinary, then my sister is a luminous example.

And so are you. When a nonreligious person spontaneously decides to navigate a devastating breakup with her heart open, her experience is sanctified. She taps an aquifer of grace and becomes a co-creator in a larger, more enlivened reality. By consciously cultivating gratitude for all the small blessings of your life, not despite but right at the core of what is hardest, you, the radiant mystic disguised as an ordinary person, emerge with a sweet aliveness you never could have imagined. Notice how external circumstances rise to meet your intention. Even if your lover has abandoned you, everything from career to other (nonromantic) relationships begins to improve, and a sense of simple wonder pervades your days. You do not need to attach God-language to this state of being. You know beyond words and concepts that something holy is happening, and all that is required of you is to show up and welcome it.

Like Amy, you will still struggle with feeling empty and alone sometimes. For an ordinary mystic, there is no fixed state of awakening, after which you never again experience pain or doubt. To be alive to the radiance and meaning enfolded in the shadow of your life is to be where you are when you are there, and to set your intention to remember and rediscover your innate connection to spirit, again and again.

Your Holy Imagination

My old friend and mentor Ram Dass had a healthy relationship with magical thinking.

"What, so you talk to your dead guru in your head?" one cynical reporter asked him.

"Yes," said Ram Dass, who by that time did not speak much, a hemorrhagic stroke having robbed him of his famous gift of gab.

"And your dead guru talks back?"

"Mm-hm."

"Isn't that just . . . your imagination?"

"Yeah!" Ram Dass agreed, beaming.

For Ram Dass, imagination was not fake, as opposed to empirical reality. Rather, imagination was a gift, one of many paths that can lead us from sorrow to joy. Hanging out with his guru in the field of his holy imagination made Ram Dass very, very happy.

It's all about intention. I intend to see my lover as an embodiment of love. I mean to bless my food before I eat it, bless the farmers who grow it and the truckers who transport it, bless the people who at the moment I am eating are suffering from the emptiness of hunger. I purposely pause in the middle of a traffic jam when I am already late for a dentist appointment and take some mindful, heartful breaths and open up a little space around my stress.

There is a word in Hebrew that encompasses this spiritual impulse: *kavanah*. It means "intention," but it's more than simply a matter of setting your sights on a goal and taking aim. It's about an alignment of the heart. When we engage in any kind of spiritual enterprise, we begin by attuning our hearts to what matters most. This saves us from empty religiosity, yes, and it is also a way to render the most ordinary activity holy. Slicing zucchini, taking out the trash, paying your internet bill. I often frame my kavanah as a question: How can I make this conversation about racism a healing thing instead of one that causes more suffering? Or, I am about to pick up my teenage granddaughter from school, and what about not taking it personally if she rebuffs my efforts to offer a bit of elder guidance? Or, what can we both discover if I walk through this door and sit at the bedside of my dying friend without an agenda? Kavanah is a marriage of purpose and receptivity. I show up, and the divine presence stands before me (or doesn't; the outcome is none of my business). That presence takes many, often surprising, forms.

This will probably come as no surprise to you: I love to invent rituals. Weddings and memorial services, baby blessings and business meetings. I light candles and incense, read a poem or play a song. I go around the room and give everyone a chance to identify something that someone they love taught to them, or one thing they'll miss when they die, or a shitty moment in their week they'd like to lay down at the feet of the divine mother. Nothing in me suffers from insecurity about being qualified to make up a ritual. Why should ordained clergy have all the fun? I write prayers for healing everything from divorce to addiction. Do I think the power of my words will change reality, or that if I fail to pray properly a negative outcome is my own damn fault? Of course not. It's that weaving a ritual to hold the magnitude of certain moments helps to infuse those moments with beauty, with wonderment. The sacred bubbles up from the innocent ground of moments like these, and I want to be there when it does.

Practice
YES, THIS, AND THAT TOO

In many mystical traditions, across the spectrum of the world's religions, we find a paradoxical teaching that says the most reliable means for knowing God is by unknowing. Christian mysticism uses the Latin term, *via negativa*. We are encouraged to actively dismiss any words or concepts to define the vast mystery of the divine, resting in what we *cannot* say about God, rather than what we think we *can* say. In Hinduism, the Upanishads introduce a method of meditative inquiry, *neti neti* ("not this, not that"), that is designed to peel away the layers of false thoughts and arrive at a bedrock of nondual awareness in which we experience our essential unity with all that is. The early twentieth-century Indian sage Ramana Maharshi suggested we ask ourselves again and again, "Who am I?" Each time we think we've landed on a true description, we let it go. Not this, not that.

I invite you to turn this stark technique on its head. While unknowing has its place on the path of awakening, it can be a disembodied practice that leads to checking out of reality (sometimes called transcendence) rather than fully inhabiting the holiness of your life.

Try this: Sit in a comfortable position with your back straight, allow your eyes to close, take a couple of deep, slow breaths, and ask yourself the question "Who am I?" Rather than responding in the negative, say yes to whatever arises. I am a mother and a daughter, a sister and a lover: *yes*. I am a cabinet-maker, a gardener, an activist: *yes*. I am a sensitive person, a drama queen, a tortured artist: *yes*. I am someone others can come to when their hearts are broken because I listen with love: *yes*. I am a part of the vast universe, no more or less important than an aspen tree: *yes*. Now, get creative: I am sunlight on water, a breeze that lifts my hair, the stillness of midnight, a symphony: *yes*.

You are all of these and beyond them all. You get to be both vast and particular, formless and gloriously made. By accepting all the scruffy and magnificent details of your human condition, and allowing seemingly contradictory things to be equally true, you banish the conditioned voice that designates some things as holy and others as profane. Set your intention to welcome every-thing you are and watch your life open like a fist, like a flower, like a gate.

✳

WRITING PROMPT:

What I really want is . . .

TWO

Attention

A Fearless Gaze

Loving Awareness

Now that you have set your intention to make yourself available to the beauty and wonder in everyday life, it's time to tune all your faculties to perceive it. Pour your attention into the vessel of the present moment. Notice its sensory details, its contours and shadows. Take notes, physically or mentally. Be present, yet not hyper-vigilant. Soften your focus so that you glimpse the vast sky behind the passing clouds. Be willing to see things as they are, and yourself as you are. This is a courageous gaze, a mystical gaze. I'm encouraging you to cultivate it.

Here's how contemplative activist and Franciscan friar Richard Rohr describes this sacred attention: "God-in-us is a riverbed of mercy that underlies all the flotsam and jetsam that flows over it and soon passes away. Vast, silent, restful, and resourceful, it receives and also releases all these comings and goings. It is awareness itself . . . To look out from this untouchable silence is what we mean by contemplation."[1]

Ram Dass called it "loving awareness." That is, it's not just a matter of being aware; it's about love. In the final years of his life, "I am loving awareness" was Ram Dass's mantra. As his life force began to slip away, I watched in hushed delight as my lifelong teacher indeed became that which he had spent so many decades teaching about. "He's becoming translucent," my friend Nina reported after visiting Ram Dass as he was nearing the end. I thought that was a better—far more vibrant and accurate—description of our mentor's ripening soul than "transparent." He was not so much disappearing as becoming a clear window through which love-light could pass.

In her mystical masterpiece *The Interior Castle*, sixteenth-century saint Teresa of Avila invites us to find the holy within: "Always visualize the soul as vast, spacious, and plentiful . . . The sun at the center of this place radiates to every part . . . God has given it such dignity."[2] Richard Rohr points out that this is so for every single one of us: The soul is God-within-you. Your True Self.[3]

----

1 Richard Rohr, *Immortal Diamond: The Search for Our True Self* (San Francisco: Jossey-Bass, 2013), 23.

2 Teresa of Avila, *The Interior Castle*, trans. M. Starr (New York: Riverhead, 2002), 45.

3 "Emotional Sobriety: A Riverbed of Mercy," Center for Action and Contemplation, June 20, 2022, https://cac.org/daily-meditations/a-riverbed-of -mercy-2022-06-20/.

Connecting to that divine presence inside you does not, I'm afraid, rescue you from the human predicament, however, lifting you to some elevated perch from which you can dispassionately observe the poor slobs suffering below. Rather, when you plant yourself in the ground of what is, your capacity to be present to all of life expands. Refining your faculty of perception allows you to feel everything, to feel deeply and even intensely, and yet also not drown in the experience. When we practice this kind of sacred seeing, we are able to perceive the world as its best, overflowing with grace. Sometimes broken grace, destabilizing and aggravating, but real and beautiful.

Luckily, you're not completely on your own here. There are age-old tools and techniques designed to help you pay attention, contemplative practices that train you to understand your mind and forge intimacy with your heart: like centering prayer in the Christian tradition; Vipassana practice in Buddhism; dhikr, or repetition of the divine names, in Islam; and many forms of meditation in Hinduism. Feel free to check them all out, study with a teacher or experiment on your own, and even make up your own methods for showing up for the full experience of the present moment. What you are doing is saying yes to a contemplative way of life.

It does not only happen when you close your eyes and sit in silence. Contemplative practice fills the cup of your mind, spilling over and splashing all the other hours, permeating your days with the fragrance of love, like sliced fruit or rain on the garden. Contemplative life slows you down enough to catch the magic that flashes from the heart of the mundane.

It helps to intentionally carve out spaces for silence and stillness.

Maybe the most effective practice for you is to unplug from your own devices, stick the kids in front of the TV, and take a walk alone on the beach, allowing yourself to stop and watch the way a sandpiper probes for food beneath the surface of the sand. Solitude peels away the layers of distractions and invites us to meet the present moment naked. External quiet helps quiet the mind, and a quieter mind is more likely to encounter what is real and true.

Friar of Love

My friend Carmen Acevedo Butcher is a translator of long-dead but ever-relevant mystics. She has taken on two of my favorite texts and rendered them in astonishingly alive language. First, she translated the *Cloud of Unknowing*, written by an anonymous medieval master (I like to imagine "Anonymous" as a woman, whose only chance of being taken seriously was to conceal her identity), in which the author poetically teaches that the most reliable means for knowing God is to unknow everything you thought you knew. Carmen's other great translation is the *Practice of the Presence*, by the French Carmelite Brother Lawrence. She calls him the "Friar of Love."

Brother Lawrence taught a deceptively simple, revolutionary contemplative method, as relevant today as ever. Maybe even more so, given that the opportunity for distraction has exponentially increased in the three centuries that have passed since the Friar of Love suggested we cultivate a habit of attentiveness to the divine presence. Brother Lawrence reminds us that every task, no matter how ordinary, is a fresh opportunity for drawing near to the "Friend." And that the more we take refuge in this intimacy, the more often we find ourselves simply resting in the presence of Love itself. All we need to do is turn inward. In the beginning, he suggests, we can say things like "'My God, I am all yours,' or 'God of love, I love you with all my heart,' or 'Love, create in me a new heart,' or any other phrases Love produces on the spot."[4] Eventually, your mind will more effortlessly land in God like a butterfly on a branch, and you will no longer need words. There are no rules. No "ought to" or "mustn't" in the Practice of the Presence. It is not even required that you subscribe to a belief in a personified deity to harvest the fruits of this intention to be lovingly present.

Brother Lawrence's story is a story of brokenness, one in which many of us can find our own faces reflected. Born Nicolas Herman into a poor family in 1614, he decided as a teenager with no prospects to join the military and fight in a war that gave him a sense of purpose and a bit of money. He endured (and possibly perpetrated) horrors he never was able to speak about and was wounded in battle, which left him with a painful limp and a severe case of what we today call post-traumatic stress disorder. Even after joining a Carmelite monastery in the hope that a life of prayer might alleviate his suffering, Brother Lawrence spent a decade, from his mid-twenties to his mid-thirties, teetering on the knife edge of suicidal despair. What kept him alive was the memory of a leafless tree he saw one winter. He knew that soon new growth would sprout from its bare branches, and it would again burst into blossom and eventually bear fruit. This gave him hope that in the deepest darkness of our souls, we could trust that a season of renewal was coming. Grappling with

---

4 Brother Lawrence, *Practice of the Presence*, trans. Carmen Acevedo Butcher (Minneapolis: Broadleaf, 2022), 54.

anxiety and depression, he instinctively began turning to Love in the midst of everyday life and centering himself there.

In the monastery, Brother Lawrence was assigned to the kitchen, a duty for which he was ill-suited. He hated cooking. He did not like chopping onions and washing big pots. He spent hours on his feet, which inflamed his injuries. As he struggled to surrender to his circumstances, his reliance on his Love practice deepened. He tried to think about God as he stirred the sauces, to speak to God as he directed his kitchen staff, to thank God as he served up bowls of onion soup to the other brothers. Remembering the divine did not come easily to the traumatized monk. But the more he cultivated this simple awareness, the easier it was to slip into the Presence. And everyone around him began to notice the change in him. Not only did he seem happier, but he became increasingly kinder. He listened more deeply to the pain of others, and just being with him made them feel better. In need of healing himself, he became a source of healing for others.

Carmen found herself inexplicably relating to Brother Lawrence. She wasn't a military veteran, and her wounds were not obvious, but, like so many of us these days, she was debilitated by anxiety, damaged by a traumatic childhood. As one of the few brown-skinned people in her Bible Belt community, Carmen did not fit into the Southern Baptist society of her youth. She suffered from undiagnosed dyslexia and attention deficit disorder, which drove her even deeper into self-isolation. Carmen often escaped into nature where she found solace amid the rivers and trees.

She still does. After decades of therapy and contemplative practice, with award-winning translations and a beautiful marriage, Carmen still needs the remedies she developed to survive. She is known for slipping out of social gatherings and bolting into the wilderness. "That's where God has always met me," she says. Her loved ones have become accustomed to Carmen's disappearances. Every day, she pulls on her rubber boots and walks in the wetlands around her Bay Area home. There, she also practices the Presence, as Brother Lawrence taught her, and as her own heart spontaneously guided her to do over decades of carrying the burden of feeling different. "I'm a student of the marsh," she says. Meaning, she cultivates a fearless gaze and pays attention.

"We all limp," Carmen tells me, "only for most of us, the wound is invisible." She reminds me about the biblical story of Jacob, who wrestled all night with an angel of God and in the morning was triumphant and was renamed "Israel." The part that people tend to forget, Carmen points out, is that Jacob's hip was dislocated in the battle and never properly healed. Like Brother Lawrence, Jacob limped for the rest of his life. But he also found the Holy One through the portal of his struggle.

As a teacher and a passionate protector of human dignity and the flourishing of the planet, Carmen feels the injustices of the world in her own body. But like the Friar of Love she so masterfully translated for the rest of us, she returns again and again to the simple remembrance of the divine, turning to love and praying for mindfulness before opening an email, asking for help with an anxious feeling, sharing her worry for a friend, or being grateful for the sunrise. Carmen does not require a church for this practice. Nor a monastery. Nor even a plan. She simply walks out into the wild morning and says, "Here I am, God. I love you." And the egrets mirror it back: "Good morning, Carmen. We love you, too."

For Carmen, contemplative practice is not only personal; it's communal. "While I was translating Brother Lawrence," she tells me, "I kept thinking, *Is this useful? Is this going to help my students who have lost loved ones to COVID? Is it practical? Will it make someone's life kinder and better?*" The answer is yes. Practicing the Presence has the power to transform everything. From the self-compassion it generates, compassion for all beings flows. We realize that God does not come to us because we dared to look. God has been here all along.

Try it. Try it right now. Put down whatever you are doing and close your eyes. Or open them. It doesn't matter. Stop talking and just listen. Expand your senses beyond the clamor of your thoughts and pay close attention to the quality of the air around you. Notice the miracle of your breath flowing in and out. The sounds of nearby birds and faraway traffic. Say something loving to the One who made you, even if you don't exactly believe in a Creator. Imagine that sacred Presence filling the space you opened by virtue of having welcomed it in. Keep it simple. Remember what this feels like. You will be coming back. Returning to Love again and again.

Grounded in Groundlessness

When I asked Reverend SeiFu, a longtime Zen practitioner, how he embodies contemplative practice in everyday life, his response was "How could I not?" Meaning, meditation has so thoroughly soaked his being that his inner landscape is permeated by it, and it splashes into every aspect of his days. "Contemplation bridges the gap between inner and outer," SeiFu tells me. "Whether I'm pouring salt or watching waves, I'm listening to eternity and it's speaking through me." This may sound extravagant, but SeiFu is one of the most grounded people I know. Maybe that's because what he's grounded in is groundlessness.

A foundational teaching of Buddhism is the truth of impermanence. But you don't need to be a Buddhist to notice that everything passes. That which you love—whether your youthful looks or a dish of chocolate mousse—will inevitably come to an end, and tedious tasks will be finished soon enough. When we hold reality in a fearless gaze, we discover that the impermanent is an invitation into the eternal. This transforms death from a catastrophe into an old friend and mundane tasks into deeper invitations. "Use every hard thing that's ever happened to you as a way to punch through to the vastness you long for," SeiFu counsels. "Till your darkness. Ferment, distill, fertilize it. New spiritual awakening will arise from that compost, I promise."

Meditation helps. "I've built a solid foundation in contemplative practice, even though it grounds me in nothing," SeiFu admits. "The impermanent is my grounding."

Can you make space in your life for this paradox? Can you loosen your grip on your bank balance and the imagined opinions of people you hope to impress? Open your fist and release the birds of blame and shame? Stop trying to get away from grief, bypass injustice with spiritual mumbo jumbo, push the boulder of regret out of the road? Sit down. Take a few deep breaths and consider allowing yourself to tumble from the cliff of certitude into the buoyant air of not-knowing. You do not have to have all this shit figured out. It is not your job to get it all under control. The invitation is to notice what comes and bless what goes. To take refuge in groundlessness and rest in boundlessness.

Unplug

Industrialized society seems to run on the vapors of exhaustion. There is always one more thing to do (or two, or ten) before we feel we deserve to take a break and refill the depleted cup of our energy. We just buy another latte or pound a Red Bull and muscle on through. The developing world has lost the power of rest. I've always considered the siesta to be a highly evolved custom. Most countries in the Global South and many Mediterranean lands roll up the sidewalks from around 2 to 5 p.m. every day. Workers go home to share the main meal of the day with their families and then lie down for a while. This recharges the batteries, yes, and it also breathes some space into life so that we can notice the quieter, sweeter, more earthy things we neglect to see when we're busy bending the world to our will.

Maybe you can't do this. You have a nine-to-five job, and no one is going to grant you the freedom to take three hours off to cook and eat a big meal, accompanied by a cold beer, and then swing in your hammock and listen to birdsong. I get that. Maybe you have a finance team to manage, a class of fifth-graders to teach, a bathroom remodel to complete. But there are ways to weave some stillness into your days. Find a quiet corner where you can take a fifteen-minute nap. Meditate. Do a few yoga poses, slowing down to breathe deeply and mindfully as you stretch. Try out some of the many apps that offer guided relaxations. Take a walk and don't check your phone for notifications.

My favorite practice for infusing contemplative space into my life is the Sabbath. I draw on a nominally Jewish version, known as Shabbat in Hebrew, or Shabbos in Yiddish. As the sun sets on Friday, I wrap up whatever I'm doing and open the gate to being. I call my family together, and we light a pair of taper candles, welcoming the Shekinah, the indwelling feminine presence of the divine, who characterizes Shabbat in the mystical tradition. This signifies the shift from ordinary time to sacred time. From sunset on Friday to sunset on Saturday, I defy the tyranny of tasks and disengage from the compulsions that drive me the rest of the week. Shoulds and shouldn'ts are banished. A sublime space is left behind when I remove obligations, a space infused with creativity, sensuality, freedom. This is why in Judaism Shabbat is considered to be a taste of heaven. It's why there is a special ritual for ending Shabbat, called Havdalah, designed to console us when we have to leave that temple of rest and return to the everyday world.

Remember: the ground of our regular life is not other than holy. But taking a full day to pause and renew helps us to recognize the presence of the sacred intertwined with the ordinary during the other six days.

I do realize that it is a privilege to observe Sabbath on a regular basis and that contemporary Western culture does not support it. I started this custom on a whim when my kids were small and I was a single mom working two jobs. To my relief and amazement, it worked. It was as if the universe miraculously expanded to contain my commitment to tending my inner life. It is the same with meditation. I have had a morning ritual for as long as I can remember. I get up, wash my face, do half a dozen sun salutations, sit in meditation for fifteen minutes, and then start the rest of my day. It's like brushing my teeth: nonnegotiable. Otherwise, I would have spiritual halitosis, and who wants to get too close to someone with bad breath? It's a matter of priorities.

Whether you cultivate a daily practice of silent sitting, a weekly Sabbath practice, a contemplative walk in a city park, or watching your breath as you're waiting for your tea to steep, making time for stillness, silence, and solitude helps open the eyes of the heart. It teaches us to observe the mind and not buy in to all our thoughts. *That co-worker didn't greet me when I walked through the office. What a bitch. No, it must be me. I must have done something to offend her. What could I have done?* The monkey mind has grabbed the reins and off you go. As if you knew what was going on inside someone else's head. As if your imagined flaws were as real as the shoes on your feet. Stop it. Slow down. Breathe deeply and look closely. When you hone your attention, the world opens and spills its most important secrets.

Conscious Culture

Raised by revolutionaries, I have always found politics perplexing. I also consider technology tedious, and business boring. I am not proud of my resistance to these vital cultural realities, and I make an effort to compensate for it by reading widely, listening carefully, and striving to be an agent of positive change. I'm up against some serious conditioning. Since I lived in ashrams as a teenager in the 1970s, my consciousness was shaped around the mistaken notion that the mundane world is illusory and the only language to be trusted is the silence of the spirit. It is my mother, Susanna, who taught me through her own example that there is nothing that isn't sacred. Business and pop culture, art and social action—these can all be vessels for the inflow of spirit.

My mom is the epitome of a conscious entrepreneur. That said, starting a business was not what she had in mind when she and my dad rejected the values of mainstream America, uprooted their young family from suburban Long Island, and embarked on a countercultural odyssey that led us to settle in the mountains of New Mexico. One day in the early 1970s, while hiking on a trail near our home in Taos, my mom ran into a local weaver and they struck up a conversation (probably after lighting up a joint, considering the times) that changed everything. The woman mentioned an isolated Zapotec weaving village in the mountains outside of Oaxaca, Mexico, where the people still lived as they had for centuries, raising sheep, carding and spinning the wool by hand, dyeing it in vats over an open fire, and weaving complex designs on large wooden looms. Ritual and ceremony were as integral to their lives as food and family. She found the people there unfailingly warm and gracious, open and creative. My mom couldn't get the story out of her head. She had to find this mythic place.

This began her love affair with the Zapotec people and their timeless weaving traditions that has endured ever since. Over time, both parties prospered. My mom's Taos gallery became a destination for lovers of Zapotec art. The people of the village went from selling a few pieces at the market in Oaxaca City to operating a thriving weaving enterprise, while remaining steadfast in their devotion to traditional values and ancient customs. Dirt paths were replaced with paved roads, donkey carts with pickup trucks, and they built a school so that the children would not have to leave home to get an education. Women, once relegated to preparing the yarns, began designing and weaving original art pieces, to great acclaim. More than material reward, deep friendships flourished. When Susanna makes her annual trips to the village, she is welcomed as a beloved relative. Her relationships with the Zapotec families she works with span three generations and are as loving and close as any of her most intimate connections. That love is the foundation of her business.

Now my younger brother, Roy, is picking up the mantle that is naturally dropping from our mother's shoulders. Roy strives to offer everyone who walks through the gallery door a meaningful experience, whether or not it ends in a sale. Our friend Andrew says that Roy reminds him of the carpet sellers in the bazaars of the Middle East. "They are the hidden Sufi masters," Andrew explains, "disguised as humble rug merchants. To buy a piece from one of these people is to receive a blessing." In Turkey, rug sellers serve tea before any money changes hands, and this is where real transaction often unfolds. In Oaxaca no one would think of engaging in business until everyone has sipped from a small clay cup of locally brewed mescal. Hospitality and commerce are entwined. The host (the seller) treats the guest (the buyer) as a revered relative.

"*Business* has become a dirty word," my mom tells me, "associated with exploitation and overconsumption, but money is simply an exchange of energy." Just as magical, just as ordinary.

My friend Kelly would agree. Kelly is an entrepreneur whose success is grounded in generosity of spirit. Ever since she can remember, Kelly has been someone who can identify gifts in others that we may not be clearly perceiving in ourselves and help us envision how to bring them into manifestation. "I have always felt that if I have something someone needs, I want to give it to them," she says. For Kelly, this is not a sacrifice. It lights her up to see that she can resolve a conundrum that is causing someone else distress. That impulse was the genesis of the boutique editing firm she created to help struggling authors birth the books gestating inside them. This is a beautiful example of "right livelihood" in Buddhism. It is about aligning your work in the world with the innate goodness of your soul.

It was Kelly who helped heal me of the unhealthy split in my psyche between money and the dharma, this masochistic notion that we should never charge for sharing spiritual resources. One day, having tea with Kelly at my kitchen table, I confessed that I was tired of being an overworked and underpaid adjunct philosophy professor, writing on the side, earning less for leading workshops and retreats than my grandkids were making busing tables at a local café and supported by a husband who had spent a lifetime working with his hands. With patience and good humor, Kelly guided me in identifying the beliefs that prevented me from earning a sustainable wage doing what I loved most—writing books and giving teachings on the poetry of the mystics. I remember the feeling of mutual elation at the end of our conversation. Kelly had fulfilled her dharma by helping alleviate my suffering in her particular way, and I could for the first time begin to imagine offering my gifts to the world without restraint, compensated generously enough so that I could afford to be as generous as I longed to be. Ultimately, by daring to envision the life I wanted, I was able to manifest it.

To live as an ordinary mystic means embracing all arenas of life as doorways to the sacred, even if the soul is never overtly mentioned. To engage consciously with business, for example, means lifting each other up instead of trampling each other in a frenetic effort to achieve more status, more money, more power. It means replacing a culture of domination with a culture of care. Which does not preclude being well compensated for doing what you love.

My friend Zee brings breathwork to BIPOC folks in corporate America. With a Harvard MBA and training as a classical violinist, Zee embodies the balance of lucid mind and wild heart. But her true gifts were invisible to the white men who dominated the business world in which she found herself. Brought to her knees by an ongoing barrage of microaggressions in the workplace—subtle and not-so-subtle suggestions that she might be receiving special treatment because she's Black, rather than her leadership being recognized as the fruit of her creative passion and commitment to excellence—Zee embarked on a quest for healing that ultimately led her to studying yoga in yoga's ancient birthplace: India.

It was in India that Zee learned timeless techniques of conscious breathing that helped her heal her exhausted body and balance her traumatized nervous system. She scooped up those jewels and brought them back to the places that had almost killed her: the halls of American capitalism. Now thousands of people who, like Zee, may have been staggering under the weight of systemic racism are learning to breathe their way through oppressive structures and into a more liberated relationship with business, thanks to Zee's willingness to stay with the pain and transform it into service.

Danielle has a similar vision. A visionary scientist and designer,

Danielle founded the Google Empathy Lab in an effort to infuse artificial intelligence with values of compassion, emotion, and relationality. Counter to the prevailing standards of the tech world, Danielle centered the messy and the mysterious. She was not so much interested in engineering solutions as in cultivating deep feelings. Her leadership in technology spaces has been revolutionary. "Can we talk about our souls here?" Danielle dares to ask. "Because a lot of us believe in them. Why are we not acknowledging this as we make stuff for billions of people on Earth? How am I to serve other people when I've only got eight drops of myself in this chair?"

Danielle is devoted to the intersection of technological innovation with the timeless wisdom of the heart. She looks to Indigenous teachings, rooted in stones and sky, in death and childbirth, in ritual and ceremony, for the essential attributes that must be woven into the development of emerging intelligence systems if the human family is not only to effectively meet the future, but to flourish on every level. For Danielle, technology in general, and artificial intelligence in particular, is less about figuring stuff out than about resting in holy unknowing.

Most of us divide the world up into left brain and right brain, analytical and intuitive, creative and practical. We hear about developments in AI and assume that robots are going to learn how to program themselves and take over the world. Artificial soldiers will initiate deadly wars. Students will lose all capacity for critical thinking because apps will write their papers and solve their personal problems. Of course we're freaked out about the future. What we don't realize is that people like Danielle are working hard and deeply to shape our collective future in such a way that spirituality and technology meet and meld. That our capacity for wonder is stronger than our craving for efficiency. That Mother Earth will always triumph over Doctor Machine.

"When it comes to technology," Danielle says, "we tend to think of everything in terms of equations and proofs, engineering and Venn diagrams rather than the inherent circles and cycles and rhythms that, of course, everything is." She points out that *silicon* is just a fancy word for *sand*. That these chips are made of the same stuff as mountains. They are the material of our own bones. They are our relatives. Silicon chips, Danielle believes, carry ancient intelligence. "For me, they're some fairy tale from the future," Danielle says. "It's a living story about how the mountains and AI come together to restore all of us in our belonging."

Politics, too, can and must be a space for awakening love. Cora is a great example of this. She entered the political arena as a child when she stood up to bullies on the playground of her elementary school in the American heartland. Cora grew up to be an advocate for accessible healthcare and an activist for restoring tribal lands to their rightful Indigenous stewards. Her desire to serve flowered from the soil of trauma. When Cora was a baby, her father was killed in a lumber mill accident, leaving her mother a widow at the age of twenty-one. Cora has always suspected that her dad would have survived if the family had lived closer to good healthcare. Her paternal grandparents were Holocaust survivors who found refuge in Colorado. Her grandpa was the executive director of the largest Jewish family services organization in the state. From early childhood, Cora developed an awareness of geopolitics and power imbalances and pledged to do whatever she could to restore wholeness to the human community and the natural world.

After earning a master's degree from Columbia and a doctorate from Oxford, Cora brought her passion for justice to the Obama White House, serving as a senior advisor on women's economic empowerment to the US State Department. Cora also discovered an untapped storehouse of wisdom and power hidden among the wives of world leaders. Amazed that no one had bothered to ask these women their opinions about much of anything, in 2009 Cora cofounded what became the Global First Ladies Alliance to help these visionary women develop and implement their own priorities. She still convenes circles of First Ladies from around the world to discuss how they can deliver critical social services to their communities and have a meaningful impact on the global family. And now Cora is running for public office, hoping to change the culture of politics from the inside, infusing a masculine-dominated arena with feminine values of lovingkindness and fearless truth-telling.

When politics, like business and technology, is rooted in love, it can be a garden for the flowering of the human spirit. Any good garden thrives with compost. It is not despite our messiness that we flourish, but through consciously converting our manure into healthy humus. We are gloriously imperfect beings. Entrepreneurs, for instance, are humans who make mistakes, who lose their way and discover new paths. The starting place for all scientific and technological development is and must be a willingness to not know. There are plenty of politicians who value the web of interconnection and are busy mending the broken world, rather than seizing power for their own aggrandizement. These are our modern-day mystics.

They are reclaiming the everyday world as holy ground and inviting us to take our seat right here.

Practice
KEEP THE SABBATH

Dedicate a day to rest and renewal. Unplug. Set aside the to-do list, resist the temptation to check (or at least to answer) email, take a long walk and a long nap. Have sweet sex (whatever that looks like for you in this season in your life). Read poetry.

In the Jewish tradition, Shabbat is the holiest of holy days, and we observe it every week. As the sun sets on Friday, we sing three blessings, over candlelight, wine, and bread. First, we light twin candles, symbolizing the meeting of ordinary and sacred time. Next, we fill a goblet with red wine (or grape juice), which stands for the intoxication of divine love that fills the heart that cries out in longing. Finally, we uncover a loaf of challah (braided egg bread), a sign of gratitude for our connection with the earth and her bounty. And then we eat a beautiful meal, prepared consciously and with love. We relax into this contemplative space until the sun sets on Saturday, when we enter the new week restored, recalibrated, reoriented toward what matters most.

Borrowing from the Jewish tradition, you may opt to join the stream of "keeping the Sabbath holy" every week from sunset on Friday to sunset on Saturday. Or maybe you choose one day a month as a Sabbath, or fit it in whenever you feel you can (although I warn you: it rarely feels like a convenient time for a busy person to take a break). Maybe you will set aside a full weekend once a season to go somewhere by yourself and turn inward, letting go of the obligations that usually boss you around. Allow this practice to take the shape of your own life. I promise, your willingness to cease from endless doing and drop into simple *being* will reward you with an increased capacity to pay attention to what is and an irresistible impulse to praise it.

ӿ

WRITING PROMPT

Take a walk, find a point of focus,
describe what you perceive in vivid detail.

THREE

Surrender

Radical Amazement

Practice Random Acts of Wonder

We have set our intention to walk as mystics, on the lookout for the wellspring of meaning streaming from the heart of our most difficult or seemingly trivial daily experiences. We have cultivated a contemplative gaze, become willing to be with things as they are. Now we open ourselves to wonder. Twentieth-century Jewish philosopher Abraham Joshua Heschel said, "Our goal should be to live life in radical amazement . . . to get up in the morning and look at the world in a way that takes nothing for granted. Everything is phenomenal; everything is incredible; never treat life casually. To be spiritual is to be amazed."

Anne Lamott calls this "practicing random acts of wonder." The start of wonder is not-knowing. I invite you to dismantle your preconceptions, to pull on the loose thread of your belief systems and let them unravel. Allow yourself to be like a child, seeing the world through fresh eyes. Instead of trying to control life by making sense of it, embrace ambiguity and paradox as being the domain of the truest things. The holy lives in mystery, in darkness, in liminal space. Not knowing isn't a problem to be solved but rather a reality to be celebrated. In Zen Buddhism, this open stance is called "beginner's mind." Cultivate it.

Even though the mystical path is characterized by mystery, it is not a lofty and esoteric matter, requiring decades of study and secret initiation rites. It is neither vague nor sloppy. In some ways, it is the truest, clearest thing. Mysticism is about union and communion with the source of all being, which is love. This fountain bubbles up from where you stand and reveals itself in the midst of your regular life. Unlike what traditional religious institutions have taught, spirituality is not about transcending the senses. To be a mystic is to say yes to your embodied experience. Find the holy in a basket of fresh-picked raspberries, in your body's capacity to deliver the almost unbearable pleasure of an orgasm, in sand or mud or long grass between your toes. Maybe you have felt the presence of the sacred mystery in moonlight on snow, while feeding goats or folding laundry, in rising before the sun and watching the world wake up. Good. This is a gateway to the realm of the ordinary mystic.

Altered

Humans seem to have a built-in thirst for radical amazement. In adolescence, it often manifests as an attraction to drugs and alcohol.

For some, this natural curiosity morphs into dependence. My father, an alcoholic with a high degree of self-reflective capacity, recognized his addiction as a misplaced desire for transcendence. His alcoholism had a spiritual root. Like Plato asserted almost twenty-five hundred years ago, my dad believed that the world most of us see is only a faint copy of a vast and astonishing universe just beyond the edges of our perception, continuously beckoning our attention. He readily admitted that alcohol was problematic. But he considered psychedelics to be the contemporary answer to that perennial invitation. He felt that hallucinogens not only give us the advantage of glimpsing boundless realms of reality, but also grant us access to enter them. But then what? "LSD can get you in the room with Christ," said iconic psychedelic pioneer Ram Dass, paraphrasing his guru, Neem Karoli Baba, "but you can't stay there."

My dad loved movies. His favorite film of all time was the 1940 Disney masterpiece *Fantasia*. Once videotapes became a thing and he could rent them, he would drop acid, alone or with friends, and watch *Fantasia* again and again. Mickey Mouse with his enchanted broom and hippos in tutus, *The Rite of Spring* and Bach's Fugue in D Minor. "Disney had to have been tripping when he made this," Dad mused. When I adopted my first child, the first present he gave her was a *Fantasia* videotape. At first, she watched it just to be polite, but eventually and miraculously (to me) it became her favorite movie too, and when she had children of her own, she carried the tradition forward.

I have always had a propensity to slip into altered states without provocation, which can be awkward and uncomfortable, so I've mostly avoided substances that enhance such states. There I'll be, frying eggs or sorting my recycling, and suddenly the veil that tucks ordinary reality into place lifts like the painted backdrop of a first-grade play and I am sucked into a much more vivid and complex reality than the one I had taken for granted only moments before. It requires all my energy to claw my way back to anything resembling regular consciousness. This used to freak me out, but now I'm more inclined to go with the slide. My spontaneous psychedelic moments may be a result of chemical imbalance, early trauma, or some combination of these factors, but I feel no need to label them as pathological. Age has taught me that slipping into altered states will not kill me. In fact, as my dad insisted, it can be a gift. At least interesting, if not enlightening.

But what interests me more than exalted states of awareness and privileged glimpses of reality are the ordinary moments that unfold every day, revealing the magic nestled inside them. Clean sheets and sudden gusts of wind, my lover's profile as he bends to pull weeds in our garden, a text from an old friend who is thinking of me, a poem I have read a dozen times that offers a new layer of beauty I had never noticed before.

Holy Hush

"Preach the Gospel always," said Saint Francis of Assisi, "and if necessary, use words."

At least legend tells us that's what he said. And I love that. I love that this prophet of sacred simplicity understood the limits of language and can remind us that the truest things cannot be uttered. Philosopher Ludwig Wittgenstein said, "Whereof one cannot speak, thereof one must be silent."[1] Teresa of Avila confessed that she thought it was better to speak *to* God than *about* him. And John of the Cross believed that God spoke only one word in all of creation, and he spoke it in silence. It is only in the silence, John taught, that we can hear it. A famous teaching of the Buddha is called the Flower Sermon. One day, surrounded by students asking questions in the forest grove where he gave his discourses, he simply held up a flower. A wise follower smiled, and Buddha named that one as his successor.

An ordinary mystic comes to treasure moments of holy hush, when, in the face of great mystery or great beauty, a sweet silence falls like rain, washing the atmosphere with vibrant stillness. Words would be not only superfluous at a time like this, but a travesty. Who needs to comment on a kiss, analyze a sunset, explain the birth of a baby while the baby is being born?

The early twentieth-century Sufi teacher Hazrat Inayat Khan said that there is only one holy book, the sacred manuscript of nature, and that everything we need to know is written there. When you are walking in the woods or sitting on a beach, exploring rock formations in the high desert or gazing up at the canopy of a redwood forest, discovering a single trillium amid the ferns or catching the trail of a meteor in the night sky, you sometimes glimpse the perfect order of all creation. In those fleeting moments, nature becomes a clear window through which you can perceive things as they are—exquisitely arranged, breathtakingly lovely—and you cannot help but recognize yourself as part of that luminous tapestry.

---

1 Wittgenstein, Ludwig. *Tractatus Logico-Philosophicus*. Routledge, 2001.

Lost and Bedazzled

As you allow the grandeur of the world to break through your habitual perceptions, your appreciation for the rest of creation grows more personal. You begin to envision the earth as a beloved relative and nurture an intimate relationship with her. You worship the body of the world. You'll do anything to make her feel safe and happy. Your holy wonder gives rise to a fierce protectiveness and a bold desire to act on her behalf. This care comes with pain. You cannot bear to see animals suffer, gas pipelines ravaging the wilderness, aquifers drying up. Your pain is in proportion to your love.

Like a Sabbath practice, connecting with the earth takes effort. Ever since I was a child, I have had an irresistible urge to wander alone by streams, in deserts and across snowfields, along beaches and through orchards. I scramble up boulders and slide down arroyos. I hike up ridges and sit beneath ponderosas. I rub sagebrush between my fingers and inhale its fragrance every time I take my daily walk through the high desert where I live. Time in nature is as essential to my well-being as sleep.

Which is ironic because I have the worst sense of direction on the planet. How could someone so bedazzled by the world be so helplessly lost in it? I climb a mountain one way and it looks completely different on the way back down. I have led friends and relatives the wrong way on paths I have taken a hundred times. Or stopped in the midst of guiding someone back from a long hike to a favorite overlook, convinced that we were on the wrong trail, when in fact that was the only path back out; it just felt wrong. I do not trust my instincts. (You shouldn't trust my instincts in such matters either.) The world enchants me, the earth captivates me, and I consistently turn left when I should have turned right. It all feels so fluid to me. Like a river that meanders and never stays the same.

I wish I could say this is okay with me, but it still causes me great angst when I try to drive out of the parking lot of a shopping center and have no idea which way to point my car. I have burst into tears more than once finding myself hopelessly turned around on city streets, along mountain trails, and in museums. Like something fundamental is broken in me, something regular people take for granted. Of course, there is no such thing as an unbroken person. We all have secret places where some faculty we are certain was properly installed in everyone else just doesn't seem to work in us. The invitation is to connect with the beauty at the heart of the wound, the gift inside the deficit, the holiness available in the hole.

I suppose I have other senses that compensate for my lack of a sense of direction. A capacity for my heart to be broken open by a coyote crossing the highway at sunset. A tendency to be silenced by the silence of falling snow. The way I feel music in the cells of my belly. A certain fearlessness in the presence of dying people and grieving people. An impulse to bear witness to suffering. To see pain as art.

Angel Wings

For me, almost everything that happens is a Big Deal. I've always been this way. I can take the most prosaic encounter and convert it into a melodrama. This used to embarrass me, leading as it can to some awkward exchanges with people who are blindsided by how I manage to turn a passing conversation with someone in the lobby of a hospital lab into an operatic baring of souls as we wait for routine blood tests. Where my husband, Jeff, will gloss over a torn rotator cuff as if it were a hangnail, for me a menopausal hot flash becomes an alchemical fire, the metaphysical implications of which I am compelled to report in breathless detail.

The summer I turned sixty, I was diagnosed with melanoma. During the proverbial routine checkup my dermatologist discovered what appeared to be a malignant mole just above my right scapula. This was quite a feat since, as I am a fair-skinned red-headed Ashkenazi Jew who burned and blistered throughout my childhood on the beaches of Miami and the mountains of New Mexico, my skin is the canvas for an array of freckles and moles and it's not easy to distinguish what's what. Knowing I have a propensity for skin cancer, Jeff sometimes stares at my back in bed and tries to map the constellations of my body, but he doesn't have a trained eye.

I entrusted myself to Dr. Devi. She was young and clever, with beautiful dark eyes and a playful spirit. She numbed my back, sliced off the spot, and sent it to the lab. I tried—I really did—not to give it another thought. A week went by, during which my mother's partner, John, who had been suffering from an undiagnosed auto-immune disorder, was having enough trouble breathing that my mom decided to drive him to the hospital in town from their home in the country. By the time they arrived, John's lungs were filled with fluid, and the doctor on duty arranged to have him airlifted to a larger facility with better resources. My mother and brother Roy planned to drive the three hours to Albuquerque and meet up with him there. Since I lived near the hospital in Taos, Mom and Roy agreed to let me cook a meal and feed them before they got on the road.

Our house is in the flight pattern for emergency helicopters, and I often pause whatever I am doing and utter a silent prayer for whoever is in that flying ambulance, and for their worried loved ones back on earth. As I was chopping vegetables, I heard the familiar sound of the propeller and realized it was coming for our John. I decided to finish getting all my ingredients prepped and then dash down the road to see John off as he boarded his life flight.

Then the phone rang.

"Mirabai? It's Dr. Devi. I have the biopsy results and I'm sorry to say, it's positive." It took me a minute to remember (a) who Dr. Devi was, and (b) what the biopsy was for.

"Positive?"

"You have melanoma."

"Melanoma."

"Yes, it's malignant."

Later, the surgeon who cut the thing out would scoff at me when I characterized my condition as cancer. "Cancer Lite," he called it. Easy for him to say. Big blond dude with a cauterizing scalpel, a long list of routine excisions every day, and a country club membership. For now, I forgot to ask any questions, such as what stage it was and what the next steps would be. I was busy. I had loved ones to bolster. My husband was out of town for work and my brother was due at the house within the hour, so I stashed this disquieting news in a compartment in my head, climbed into my car, and drove the three blocks to the hospital.

I arrived just as they were wheeling John out of the double doors on a stretcher, and I got to grab his hand and jog beside him while they bumped him across the gravel parking lot to the helipad. My mom, always calm in a crisis, walked in stately procession behind us while I murmured inaudibly beneath the sound of the spinning rotors and tried singing a Tibetan chant to honor John's Buddhist lineage.

"I love you!" I blurted out as they lifted him from the gurney and stuffed his long limbs into the tiny compartment. I had never before proclaimed my love for my mother's lover, nor had I particularly felt it, but in that moment, it was true and I wanted him to know it in case he didn't make it through this crisis.

The helicopter wobbled into the sky while I clutched my mom's hand between both of mine as we watched it get smaller and smaller and finally disappear. We went home to meet up with Roy, and I fed them and sent them on their way, in accordance with my tidy little plan. Only then did I let myself take in my doctor's phone call.

She mentioned surgery. Immediate surgery. That someone would call me to set it up. It was Friday, and I didn't expect to hear from anyone till Monday, so I called Jeff as he was driving home, discharged my anxiety, and we settled in to wait. Meanwhile, John's lungs were drained and he was released from the hospital in Albuquerque. Our family was letting out its breath, so I didn't mention my diagnosis. It burned like a secret ember, emanating a quiet fragrance.

That weekend was vaguely psychedelic. I tried not to focus on intrusive thoughts and instead to be as present as I could be to the world around me. Colors became more vibrant, music more deeply moving, life as it is just enough and not a bit too much. It was an easy enough practice to maintain for a couple of days while I waited for the workweek to resume so we could get on with the task of getting that cancer out of me. Monday went by without a call. Tuesday flowed into the rest of the week, and by Friday my composure was starting to waver. I called my dermatologist's office, but she was out sick with a cold. The second weekend was less magical. Even though I knew better, I googled. I read all about how deadly melanoma could be, how urgent it was to have the malignancy removed before it could metastasize. I scrambled up the worry ladder, and Jeff tried to talk me down. I found a sketchbook and a set of colored pencils in a drawer and began to write and draw my way to equanimity, as I have done since early adolescence when my mind starts spiraling into turmoil.

By the time the surgeon's office finally called, I had traversed the landscape of not-knowing and had made friends with it. I had emerged with a sense that I had gained provisional access to an invisible circle of countless others who had navigated the mystery of cancer, finding a way to flourish even in the shadow of their possible impending demise, neither pushing the fear away nor allowing it to define the whole of their experience. It was simultaneously a deeply private experience and one that made me feel more connected to the rest of humanity.

No one on my medical team took responsibility for letting me slip through the cracks.

The surgeon blamed the dermatologist. "We didn't even know you existed till today," the receptionist informed me, which did nothing to reassure me that I was in good hands. "Devi should have scheduled you immediately!"

The dermatologist blamed the surgeon. "They didn't call you for over a week?" She was incensed. "You should have had that excision by now. We have no time to waste!" Again, not comforting.

The soonest they could get me in was the end of the following week, and so I settled back into liminal space and began to explore it. I could die. Or I could merely have a chunk of my back removed, gather whatever lessons were there to be learned, and get on with my life. As I sat with the full range of possible outcomes, I found myself less concerned than curious. I began to view the diagnosis as an invitation, wrapped in layers of packaging, and I took my time unwrapping it. For the previous ten years or so, I had felt like I was on a fast-moving train and some kind of force field was preventing me from jumping off. Speaking invitations, writing projects, nonprofit boards, siblings and kids and grandkids taking their turns through a revolving door of need. I was about to launch a year-long program online with my friend Andrew. We had 150 students signed up. I called him to discuss the situation.

"My darling, we must postpone! Your health is far more important than any teaching commitment."

"Andrew, I cannot do that." The thought of leaving all those people hanging was unbearable. Disappointing people felt more fatal than a cancer diagnosis.

The next thing I knew Andrew had called our mutual friend Caroline, a renowned medical intuitive, who informed me that she saw me hooked up to tubes in a hospital fighting for my life unless I canceled everything I had agreed to for the next six months.

That got through my good-girl shield.

Breaking all those promises turned out to be one of the most liberating experiences of my life. And everyone—every single person I had agreed to do something with and for—was understanding, loving, generous.

The surgery was more invasive than I had imagined. They cut deep and wide to make sure they extracted all the microscopic roots. I had thirty stitches on the outer layer and fifty underneath. I spent the next few weeks reading and dozing in the sun, eating other people's cooking, and continuing to write in my journal, illuminating pages of words with childlike art. In a spontaneous effort to visualize my healing, I sketched an image of my back, broad shoulders tapering to a sensual waist, flowing auburn hair. A winged heart appeared between my shoulder blades. Angel wings! I colored it in, shading the curves of the heart with greens and gold, detailing the feathers of the wings with purple and orange. I fell in love with my wound.

It turns out, the melanoma was the earliest stage, and although the surgery felt a bit like squashing a mosquito with a sledgehammer when the palm of a hand would have been sufficient, I was grateful to put it behind me (haha). If I am being honest, I have to admit that my old habits of overcommitting have come slinking in the tiniest crevasses and I have to beat them back, but I'm quicker to catch them now and shoo them out. I have often heard cancer survivors describe their experience as the most beautiful thing that ever happened to them. That it heightened the unutterable preciousness of this fleeting incarnation. It peeled the veneer off the surface of life and revealed a world dipped in melted gold. It brought out the most loving and generous urges in family and community. People dropped everything and showed up with pots of soup and podcast recommendations. I get it now. While my diagnosis barely qualifies, it did grab me by the hand and pull me into a sacred landscape. It was a mystical experience.

Tiny and Huge

There is nothing like a glimpse of vastness to zoom you into the smallest version of yourself. By small, I do not mean you don't matter. I mean you realize that you're an infinitesimal particle belonging to the whole of the cosmos. Lying beneath a clear night sky in August while the Perseids shoot across. Hiking to a waterfall in the jungle. Jumping off a cliff into a volcanic pool. Listening to waves crashing during a storm. Nature is a belly dancer revealing her magnificence veil by veil. And there are other moments when we are taken to our knees by radical amazement. Witnessing the birth of a baby; all that pain followed by the sense that you have been present for the return of the messiah. The last breaths of a loved one—it is so hard to die—and the holy hush that washes over the space where only minutes before a soul inhabited the now emptied-out body. The strange thing about such moments is that we are happy to feel our own nothingness. Relieved, even thrilled.

Neuroscience tells us that when we experience awe, our default mode network (DMN) grows quiet. This network is the seat of the monkey mind, that habitual mental impulse that chases after every banana of thought that pops up. It can be especially active when we are between tasks. The DMN is linked to our sense that we are an individual somebody, up against all the other individual some-bodies in this world. When it is stilled in the wake of wonder, our awareness opens to the rest of creation. We turn our attention to the needs of the collective, and we spontaneously wish for the well-being of others.

The compassion awakened in the heart of the amazed is not fluffy. It is like a deep, still pool. Studies show that people who ex-perience awe have an increased capacity for critical thinking.[2] At the same time that your empathy is stimulated, your bullshit detectors are lit up. You are less likely to be manipulated by empty arguments and political rhetoric. When your mind is blown and your heart ex-pands, your humility deepens. You become aware that the world is magical, mysterious, and heartbreaking. You know that you know nothing, really, and this is not a problem. It's a cause for celebra-tion. Ambiguity, paradox, and darkness are the domain of wonder. You are honored to visit.

Not only does awe diminish the ego, it slows down time. This does not mean you live longer when you experience radical amazement. It means that your sense of the linear passing of the minutes is suspended in the face of an awe-inspiring experience. You are catapulted into the present. All the meditation practice in the world may not yield the power of presence into which you

---

2 Summer Allen, "Eight Reasons Why Awe Makes Your Life Better," *Greater Good Magazine*, https://greatergood.berkeley.edu/article/item/eight_reasons _why_awe_makes_your_life_better.

plunge when you stand on the gorge bridge and gaze down at the Rio Grande far below, or ski fresh powder or surf a monster wave. Lovemaking can be just as potent, or making art, or watching a stoic man break down at his father's funeral. Bearing witness to the most naked moments of the human condition rescues you from the prison of individualism and sets you free in the vast cosmos, your true home.

Education

The classroom can be a crucible for awe. But, in the United States at least, it rarely is. Our school systems seem to be designed to produce obedient cogs for the machinery of consumerism. Standardized tests demand conformity and squelch quirkiness. Atypical learners slip through the cracks and disappear, often concluding (erroneously) that they are deficient, rather than unique and wondrously made. Children are allowed to be creative through kindergarten, after which they are expected to read what they are assigned, write in response to inane scenarios, and memorize facts that have been scrubbed of surprise. Funding for art and music programs has dwindled while addiction to social media has skyrocketed.

In early adolescence, I managed to sidestep the expected trajectory of public education in this country. I had the good luck of attending an alternative school where the model of the "whole child" prevailed. It was 1973 and I had just turned twelve. My family had recently settled in the mountains of New Mexico, home to a magical little school called Da Nahazli ("Return of the Spring" in

Diné Bizaad, or the Navajo language). Naomi and Jeff Tatarsky, the founders of our educational utopia in Taos, were British intellectuals dedicated to nurturing children's bodies, minds, and spirits. They believed that adults should not impose prepackaged ideas of what every student should know, but rather listen carefully to what the child is drawn to and support that.

As it turned out, what most of us were drawn to was art. Sketching and painting, pottery and embroidery. We made poster poems, composing our verses on large pieces of white cardboard and illustrating them with magic marker borders. Every wall of the converted adobe hacienda that housed our school was decorated with children's art. We learned folk dances from all over the world, sang traditional songs from every culture, wrote musical plays and performed them for the community, acted out incisive parodies of the adults in our lives. We formed bands or played solos. If we felt like balancing equations or working on geometry proofs, the math corner was made as appealing as possible. Our playground was a wonderland of hand-built activity stations where we could exert ourselves to our youthful limits and hone our full-body co-ordination, as well as secret groves where we could engage each other in make-believe games, which sometimes lasted for months, becoming more elaborate with each iteration. Cozy "listening sta-tions" were set up in the corners, where we could slip on a pair of headphones and be surrounded with Mozart concertos or Indian ragas while we read.

When I turned fourteen, I aged out of Da Nahazli. I could have attended Taos High, but I felt like an alien in the mainstream. I could not relate to pep rallies and makeup techniques. I had no aptitude for memorizing facts and regurgitating them on multiple-choice tests. In a traditional setting, I looked deficient at best, learning-disabled at the extreme. I did not wear the right clothes. My skin smelled of patchouli and wood smoke. My family did not own a television. All I wanted to do was write short stories and paint abstract watercolors. And read. And read and read! Mostly literary fiction, favoring women's voices, but also spiritual texts, both ancient and contemporary.

I dropped out and followed friends to Mendocino, California, to work on an organic farm. I was in charge of the goats. I fed them and milked them, and I also talked to them. And I listened to them, gazing into their jasper-colored eyes, tuning to their singular personalities, appreciating their intelligence, and troubleshooting solutions to their mischief-making, such as nibbling the bark off all the fruit trees. I made cheese with their fragrant milk and baked whole-wheat bread to spread it on. I did not go to school.

Until one day a couple of young guys with long hair tumbling out of their baseball caps came rumbling up the dirt drive in a VW bus and asked whether any teenagers were living on the farm, and were they by chance enrolled in high school? I couldn't decide whether to hide, lie, or come clean. They seemed harmless, even familiar—as if they could have been part of my parents' counter-culture circle back home in Taos—so I listened to their proposition.

They introduced themselves simply as Chuck and Jeff. It turns out, they were driving all over Mendocino County on a mission to find high school dropouts. Jerry Brown, the governor of California, had recently funded an alternative educational program to support kids like me who did not fit into the mainstream model. It was built around independent studies and apprenticeships, a kind of teenage version of my earlier education that took its cues from what turned kids on, rather than imposing a standardized framework.

"Could I get credit for working on the farm?" I asked.

"You can!" Chuck responded. "If you submit a weekly farm journal."

"I've always wanted to write and illustrate a fairy tale," I announced.

"Perfect. Here's a book that may inspire you." And Jeff handed me a copy of *The Hero with a Thousand Faces* by Joseph Campbell.

"How about a deep study of an ancient Tibetan text with me?" suggested Chuck. "You seem to have a spiritual vibe." He nodded to the mala I was wearing around my neck, a string of 108 beads used for mantra practice in the Hindu tradition, given to me by my teacher, Ram Dass.

"Sure," I said.

"We could hook you up with an immersion in conversational Spanish," Jeff offered.

"Yes," I said. Yes, yes, to all of it. Music and art, philosophy and geology, social action and meditation.

I spent a year in this school-within-a-school, on the far edge of a football field, nestled on the Mendocino headlands overlooking the Pacific Ocean. At first, I would go in for half a day each week, which turned into two, then a full day on Mondays, Wednesdays, and Fridays. I met other creative, artistic, introspective kids, many of whom, like me, were living on their own, working in cafés and on fishing boats, trying to survive. At the end of the Community

School program, I took the California High School Proficiency Exam and graduated at age sixteen with a certificate of equivalency.

By the beginning of the following year, I was teaching yoga and drama there. I directed plays and published a student-run literary and arts magazine. I started taking community college classes and accumulating credits. When I was nineteen, I returned to my home state to study anthropology at the University of New Mexico in Albuquerque. High school had not been for me, but I loved college. It was like a buffet of ideas. Some were delicious and soul-satisfying and I gorged on them; others were dense and dull and I endured them. I drifted over to the philosophy department for graduate school and wrote my master's thesis on the Spanish mystics, whom I had fallen in love with while studying Spanish literature in Seville, Spain, during my junior year abroad.

My first real job was teaching at a private high school in Palo Alto, California, for gifted kids in trouble, either with drugs, crime, mental illness, or, in many cases, some toxic soup of all three. Being in my early twenties, of small stature, and looking younger than my years, I had trouble projecting authority. But I didn't have trouble connecting with my students as real people. I listened to them. I played my guitar and sang Leonard Cohen songs for them. I opened to them a treasure trove of my favorite fiction and poetry. I led them in Natalie Goldberg's writing practice exercises, and their own voices astounded them; it's all they wanted to do. I arrived at school early each day, laid out a circle of mismatched cushions, and invited anyone who felt like joining me to a half hour of silent meditation. Our gathering grew until we filled the edges of my classroom.

New Mexico kept calling me home. I wanted to create a place in my own community where kids who did not fit into the standard educational model could flourish. I returned to my hometown of Taos and cofounded an alternative high school rooted in the values instilled in me at Da Nahazli when I was a child, which had flourished at the Mendocino Community School when I was a teenager and which had nourished my students in Palo Alto. Working with a small team of visionary educators, we founded Chamisa Mesa High School. We centered the curriculum on wilderness education and creative arts and made sure the academics were rigorous enough that our graduates could attend any college they aspired to. We had a makeshift recording studio where the students worked directly with professional musicians. Working artists taught every medium in a studio filled with donated supplies, and published authors led writing workshops. We started every day gathered in the adobe great room, holding hands in a circle and taking three deep breaths together. We empowered the kids to govern themselves, and they took their leadership seriously. As a result, there were almost no disciplinary issues in our diverse school community.

What moved me most was the love. Not only the way my heart welled up with affection and admiration for the beauty, creativity, and wisdom of our students. Not only the way they trusted and treasured us, their teachers. It was their love for each other. It was how they created community and let themselves down into the safety of that collective container. The world is a perilous place, and when you are a teenager, the intensity is magnified. Watching those kids arrange themselves in giant puppy piles during morning meetings, making each other tea and toast in the school kitchen, or braiding each other's hair on the sunny porch, I knew we were leaving the world in good hands.

Believe me, I do recognize that my educational experience was unusual, both as a student and as a teacher. But I'm convinced that any classroom can be transformed into a temple if we enter it as sacred space. We cannot wait for an invitation from the academy, whose structures and systems are designed to maintain the status quo, keep things superficial and predictable, minimize innovation and epiphany. But possibilities for mystical experience are everywhere—in calculating yearly rainfall patterns and in reading the collected works of DWM (Dead White Men); in programming video games and in shooting hoops out back; in the abundance of words and in the silence that flames up between them.

I am not advocating that we entirely dismantle the public school system. I have the heart of a disrupter, but I don't have the bones of an insurrectionist. What I am calling for is a collective effort to reanimate the industrialized curriculum with our wild imagination, with enchantment and play, with the poetry of great ideas and the artistry of self-expression. With love. We can do this as a community of educators and administrators, parents and students, plus an ingathering of caring others. We can commit to being lifelong seekers of knowledge, within and beyond the classroom.

Reclaim with me now the holy ground of learning. Open the gate and invite our children to enter the garden that society has accidentally placed off-limits. And you: Rewild your own brain. Take up the study of a subject you don't think you have time for, maybe something you never thought you had aptitude for. French or astronomy, Islamic theology or existentialism. Our minds are vast, capable of delivering doses of life-altering magic. To be a true teacher and an ever-engaged seeker of wisdom is to be a revolutionary. This means unlearning everything we thought we knew about education and returning to a state of childlike wonder.

Letting Go

Sometimes when I am wrestling with a problem or a decision, I remember that I don't have to figure it out. I can give it over. My default is to the Great Mother. I murmur words like these: "Here, Mama, you take it." And then I get on with my day and wait to see what happens. It does not escape me that there may or may not exist some external divine feminine being who receives my burdens when I offer them up to her. But that doesn't matter. The very act of surrender loosens the knot, and I can breathe again. The space that opens around the issue almost always allows a good solution to enter.

Say I have received an invitation to fly to some beautiful place to teach a workshop with someone I love. But I already have three events booked the week before and two afterwards. Could I cram in this additional lovely thing? I could. Should I? Probably not. My soul needs fallow time. My body needs to curl up with a good novel and a bowl of salted nuts. My mind needs to focus on one or two things at a time, not ten. As I weigh the pros and cons, I find myself getting more agitated and less clear. Then I remember. Hand it over to Her. Within minutes, an idea for a person to take my place reveals itself like a mountain peak emerging from a bank of clouds. I call up my friend, let her know how much I would have loved to do this thing I am declining, and recommend the other teacher. "Yes," my friend says. "I'd rather have you, but that does sound like a good fit."

The heart of the matter is surrender. You surrender to the mystery, because I don't care how sharp your intellect, you can't figure this all out with your mind. The beauty, the heartbreak. The Great Mystery is meant to be revered, not solved. In Islam, the most misunderstood and maligned religion in America, the entire goal is surrender. The word *Islam* is sometimes translated as "the peace that comes with surrender to God" and comes from the same root as the word *salaam*, "peace." You don't have to be a Muslim (or even believe in God) to experience the serenity that washes over you when you give up the struggle—whatever your version of the struggle may be in any given moment—and submit to reality. It helps if you can envision reality as benevolent. As Love Itself. Use your holy imagination!

Practice

MANTRA

Find a sacred word or phrase to use as the touchstone of meditation. You can draw it from your own language, like *Peace* or *May I walk in wonder*. Or you can borrow a sacred word or mantra from one of the world's great holy languages, such as *Shalom* in Hebrew or *Om mani padme hum* in Sanskrit.

I like to use a string of prayer beads for this practice, such as a mala (108 beads, used in the Hindu and Buddhist traditions), a tasbih (99 beads, the Islamic tradition), or a rosary (59 beads, the Catholic tradition). Any beads of even shape, large enough to feel between your fingers, will do; it doesn't need to have religious significance. You are an ordinary mystic! You know how to find the sacred in everything!

Hold the beads between the thumb and index finger of one hand. Sit comfortably, with your spine straight, and allow your eyes to close or simply lower your gaze. Begin to move the beads from one finger to the next, silently uttering your mantra with the touch of each bead. When you arrive back at the starting place, turn the string of beads in your hand and begin again, moving the other way. Take your time. There is no rush. See if you can heighten your awareness of your breath as you repeat your mantra. One of my favorites is *Sita Ram*, a Sanskrit mantra that invokes the balance of masculine and feminine energies.

Another option is to simply sit in the silence for a minimum of ten minutes and remember your sacred word or phrase from time to time, using it as an anchor when your thoughts drift away. Try *Be still*, or *May all beings be well*. This method is known as centering prayer in the Christian contemplative tradition. Rather than continuously repeating a divine name or special prayer, you engage the sacred word or phrase as a lure you toss into the waters of your consciousness from time to time to lead you back home to your heart.

What's interesting is that the more you practice the repetition of a mantra or centering prayer, the more these sacred words weave their way into your consciousness. You may find yourself silently chanting *Om Namah Shivaya* on the subway as you make your way home from work or waking up in the morning with *Mary full of grace* running through your body like a warm current of mercy.

✻

WRITING PROMPT

I am amazed . . .

FOUR

Transmission

At the Feet of the Masters

You Are a Master

Let's get this right out of the way: I don't really even believe in masters. Not as some perfected versions of humankind, paragons of excellent qualities to which ordinary mortals like you and me might as well not even dare to aspire. We are all great at something, and our greatness usually lines up with our love. Do you enjoy making omelets? Then it's probably easy for you and you're probably good at it. There. You qualify as an omelet master! Maybe you have discovered the art of haiku. You have a knack for distilling the quintessence of the natural world into three potent lines that manage to convey the entire meaning of life in a brief description of a chicken feather floating in a trough of water. You, my friend, are most likely a haiku master.

This is not to say that geniuses like Etta James or Frida Kahlo are not worthy of being lifted as luminaries. They light our way as musicians and artists. Exploring ancient gnostic texts and contemporary BIPOC song lyrics changes the way we see the world, and for the better. When we read insightful writers, listen to evocative music, look at great works of art, we receive a boon, and it enlarges our capacity for encountering the sacred. Like any good guru, it wakes us up. The world needs more awakened people.

There is a reciprocal relationship between those who awaken and those who wake us up. In India, the guru gives *darshan*, that is, through her presence, she transmits an energy that transforms those who sit with her. This transmission not only lifts and shifts consciousness, but fills the heart, and then the heart naturally spills over with devotion. You think the guru is immune to your devotion? Unlikely. Your love affirms that by showing up for what she has been called to do and be in this lifetime, she is aligning with her true purpose. It is the exchange of love that matters here. Not the personalities, not the power dynamics.

One of my favorite modern mystics is Anandamayi Ma (1896–1982), who, in gentle defiance of centuries of tradition in India, did not turn to a recognized guru (that is, a man) to sanction her spiritual attainment. She took her seat in her own throne of awakening and initiated herself. Anandamayi Ma ("Bliss-Permeated Mother") taught that everyday acts, undertaken with awareness and infused with love, bring us into harmony with the universe. Sometimes she taught through words, often through silence, and always through her simple example of living a life rooted in the heart.

Although I am excited about dismantling the inherited hierarchies defining who qualifies as a saint and the 99 percent of the rest of us relegated to the ranks of the unenlightened, I don't want to accidentally fire the wisdom-keepers who have dedicated their lives to dispelling illusion and alleviating suffering in this world. Revered sages like Clare of Assisi and Neem Karoli Baba, activist-theologians like Howard Thurman and Vandana Shiva, and musical artists like Tina Turner and Trevor Hall mine the jewels concealed in the shadows of the human condition and lift them to the light. We respond to these masters because of the mastery imprinted in our own souls. We recognize the magic in them because it mirrors the magic in us. They remind us not only who we could be, but who we already are. All we need to do is train our gaze to the beauty they are pointing to and weave it into the tapestry of our days. A great soul can animate your blueprint for greatness. A wise being can reawaken your inherent wisdom. A person who is very loving can open the way for you to have a direct experience of love.

Refugee

I am not a plumber. I am not an opera singer or a climate scientist. I am a writer. It's all I have ever wanted to be. Writing blends my favorite things: distilling ideas to their quintessence, celebrating the beauty of language, and sitting alone in my room for hours. I long ago abandoned any pretense of portraying a finished and polished version of myself through my words. I offer what is most intimate and alive. I try to tell the truth. And I don't get to be attached to the outcome. Although I receive messages from readers whom my work has touched, I will never know the impact of my books on most people who read them. Nor do I need to. But recently, I was given the gift of discovering that something I wrote accompanied a stranger through a dark, dark night and helped her find beauty and hope in the midst of devastation.

Near the beginning of Russia's war against Ukraine, our friends Kamila and Justin were on their way to Eastern Europe so that Kamila could introduce her fiancé to her family in the Czech Republic. They flew into Prague, hoping to find a way to be of service while they were there to the refugee community fleeing the violence in neighboring Ukraine. They did not have a plan. They were not affiliated with any organization and they had no contacts. Letting intuition guide them, they headed for the train depot. In the Burger King inside the station, they met Polina.

It was early evening and the place was packed; there was no-where to sit. In a far corner, at a table for four, a young woman with brightly colored red hair tumbling from beneath a stocking cap sat by herself, hunched over a paper cup of coffee. Not wanting to assume her nationality, Kamila asked in English if they could join her. The woman gestured for them to sit. Kamila took a chance and inquired where she was from.

"Ukraine," she answered. Kamila and her fiancé exchanged a quick smile. In that moment, they knew they were exactly where they needed to be.

Kamila has a quality of tender strength and grounded presence, the ripened fruits of her own painful childhood in the Soviet Bloc. As the couple offered the young woman their unconditional regard and Kamila probed more deeply into her circumstances, Polina's reserve began to melt and her story spilled out. She was in her twenties, an aspiring artist with her whole life beckoning when war broke out in her country. Her parents had encouraged her to leave Kyiv and find refuge with a friend in Germany where her career could flower, safe from the dangers of a country under siege. With almost no money or possessions, Polina fled. And now she was wondering why. How could she leave her family behind? This did not feel like liberation. It felt like a great weight, and she could hardly carry it. It was only a week since the first Russian air strikes. She was alone, far from home, disoriented and exhausted. Kamila's soft and soothing words helped Polina lay down the yoke of guilt she was carrying and consider the possibility that there might be something beautiful ahead, some luminous meaning behind this storm of chaos.

In her backpack, Kamila happened to be carrying a copy of my book *Wild Mercy*, translated into Russian. When the conversation with Polina drew to a close and they had exchanged contact information, Kamila spontaneously handed the book to Polina. "Maybe there is something in here that will help," she said. As it turns out, it did. *Wild Mercy* became Polina's companion on her harrowing journey as a refugee. She sat up all night reading in the quiet depot, waiting for the train to Berlin. She sent a message to the couple a few days later to let them know the book had profoundly affected her. When they returned to the States and told me about their experience with Polina, I had the urge to connect with her myself. They let me know that I could find her on Facebook, and so I reached out. Polina speaks multiple languages and was trained as an English teacher, so she wrote back in English.

"I'm persuaded that the book, it's like the wand in Harry Potter.

It chooses you somehow, not the other way around," she said. "It was a magical act of the universe." Polina told me that from the first page, she felt a connection to me. I had written about cutting onions for dinner, about the full moon rising, about dissolving into the beauty of an ordinary moment. *She is just like me*, Polina said to herself, *finding beauty in details others are too busy to notice*. She admitted to me that sometimes the beauty is almost too much to bear. But knowing I too bore it gave her hope.

"I am not a religious person," she told me. "But I missed my family so much, and the book gave me warmth, like when you're all together in the living room at night and someone tells you an interesting story. You're sipping wine in a cozy armchair, listening. I felt like I was at home, even though I was sitting alone in a bus station in another country. That's how your book saved my night and brought me such desired relief."

It was not prescriptions for rarified mystical practices and descriptions of transcendental states that touched her. It was the ordinariness of my life as the narrator. "I could see the portrait of you," she said. "A woman who dances when she is happy. A woman who can listen to the morning wind and feel the flow of the day. A woman who is synchronized with the universe." Polina identified with my humanity, and it made her feel less lost. "It is not only my story that is important," she said, "but the felt emotions your story stirred in me."

Polina's story is, of course, important. The stories of anyone trying to escape violence and persecution, looking for refuge and a better way of life, deserve to be told, especially among those of us in the United States who live in comfortable oblivion. But if the ordinariness of my own life on the page gave this young woman comfort as she was fleeing war, grieving her separation from her family and community, wondering whether she had done the right thing to leave, then that's the kind of magic I'm interested in—the everyday miracles that unfold when we dare to open to the possibility of the miraculous, hidden in the dense foliage of the darkest circumstances. By reading my book and responding from her brave and vulnerable heart, Polina gave me a treasure for which I am unspeakably grateful.

I would not conceive of myself as a master, but that night I became a luminary for a young woman whose world had been plunged into darkness. You, too, are a source of illumination, in ways you may not ever guess.

Words

An everyday mystic is always on the lookout for what is true, what is beautiful, what breaks open the husks of conventional perception and sanctifies the imagination. Read everything: Latin American fiction and the *Tao Te Ching*. The *New York Times* and *The Big Book of Alcoholics Anonymous*. Walt Whitman and adrienne maree brown. Slow it down. Contemplate a page, read on, go back. As a child, I was a ravenous reader. I won the contest at the public library every year: I checked out the most books during summer vacation and consumed them all. Since television was verboten in our hippie house, books were our primary form of entertainment. And I was the designated reader. My siblings and their friends would crowd onto my loft bed, and I would read aloud from *Watership Down* and

Pippi Longstocking, Shel Silverstein poems and the grim fairy tales of the Brothers Grimm.

It wasn't until graduate school, when I was studying philosophy, that my pace changed. Trying to decipher Aristotle's *Metaphysics* or apply Immanuel Kant's categorical imperative to my own moral decisions took every ounce of attention I could muster. But then, even the dry and opaque pages from the Canon of Dead White Guys revealed their luminescence. Reading ancient Buddhist texts permanently transformed the way I read anything else. Words have become like artisanal chocolates. First I inhale their fragrance, then I contemplate the ingredients, and finally I take a bite and let it melt on my tongue before swallowing.

Every morning before meditating, and usually at least once on Shabbat, I open a poetry book and read a couple of pieces. Sometimes it is book of poems by an ecstatic Sufi mystic, and other times it is an anthology of Native voices from the Americas. It may be medieval or contemporary, naturalist or nondual. I say yes to it all. And when something electrifies me with its wisdom or beauty, I save it to read again later, and share it at family dinners or as a kind of invocation for a class I may be teaching. Teresa of Avila admits that she would no sooner dare to sit down to meditate (she called it contemplative prayer) without something to read than she would enter a battlefield without a shield. The explosion of thoughts would never give her peace. But if she had a book beside her, it would settle her mind and allow her to slip into states of deep stillness, what she deliciously calls the "Prayer of Quiet." She says she didn't even need to open it!

I came of age in an anti-intellectual spiritual culture and was doubly indoctrinated by parents who rejected formal education for the same reasons they shunned organized religion. My mom felt that the public school system and most universities produced capitalist drones, fostered elitism and classism, and led people away from the deeper values of creativity and compassion. My spiritual communities preached a similar revolutionary gospel. A popular trope among the Hindu, Buddhist, and Sufi circles I sat with as a young woman was "You can't find it in the pages of books." *It* being God, or Truth, or Ultimate Reality. I could not argue with this back then, and I still can't.

And yet, can't you think of at least a half-dozen books or poems or essays that shifted and shaped everything about the way you engage your soul, seek the divine, glimpse the numinous? Certain books I read during my youth—*Autobiography of a Yogi, Siddhartha, Zorba the Greek, Their Eyes Were Watching God, The Good Earth*—flung open the gates to a landscape I can only describe as holy, granting me lifelong access.

I invite you to revitalize your commitment to reading, as if you were renewing your wedding vows in a marriage where the lights may have dimmed. There is a tension—a paradox—for me when I think about where we gain real wisdom. Is it lived experience, or is it the distilled transmission from books or scriptures? My answer most days is: both. Contemplative life will always transform us, but so will our teachers in the many forms they take. So read classic and contemporary novels, memoir and poetry, sacred scriptures and social criticism. Harvest the wisdom of the ones who walked before us, and of those who are living right now, grappling with the same issues that we are, with an open mind and courageous heart. Don't neglect voices from the margins. Follow their breadcrumbs home to love; use everything you can find as a battering ram to break down the door to the divine encounter. If you are what you eat, then in reading the mystics you become one.

Sounds

Listen to music; make music. Chant in every sacred language, alone and with others. Collect the special songs that move you most. Share them with others. Open your musical horizons and seek out styles and artists you may not have been drawn to in the past. If you are a lover of classical music, listen to hip hop. If your default is Van Morrison, tune in to traditional Persian folk songs. Do call-and-response chanting with Krishna Das or Deva Premal. Try Taizé. Belt out gospel and call out to Tara, the bodhisattva of compassion. Allow your heart to soar on the wings of song. Turn it up and dance.

When I was a child, traveling with my family in a camper around the United States and Mexico, we had a soundtrack that rippled through the movie of our road trip. The Beatles' *Abbey Road*, Cat Stevens's *Teaser and the Firecat*, Janis Joplin's *Pearl*, the Moody Blues's *Every Good Boy Deserves Favour*. We listened to Santana and Peter, Paul, and Mary; Willie Nelson and Buffy Sainte-Marie. I cannot hear "Here Comes the Sun" without picturing my mother swinging in a hammock between two coconut palms on a deserted beach in the Yucatan (that has since been developed into a high-rise beach resort). "Blue Eyes Crying in the Rain" makes me cry myself. And in a recent work of autobiographical fiction, I named a character McGee after Janis Joplin's Bobby McGee. For my parents, music was political. It expressed their deepest ideals of a new way for humans to live in society. For me, music was cellular. Songs were the fibers that connected my parts and wove the tapestry of who I was to become.

Obviously, I am not alone. Most of us love music. We breathe it like air and it sustains us like oxygen. For our earliest ancestors, music was bound up with storytelling, which in turn was bound up with spiritual life. Yet, many of us simply consume music and do not dare to make it. Everyone can sing, my friend Jenny Bird insists. Jenny is a brilliant singer-songwriter whose voice is a magic carpet that could transport the most jaded listener into the heights of ecstasy. She also teaches singing. Jenny has an ability to get an entire room of nonsingers singing their hearts out, and often in three-part harmony. This is because she believes in us. Believes that every body has been fashioned by the Great Mother to be an instrument for Her beautiful breath. All we have to do is open to the flow.

Chanting has always been one of my primary spiritual practices. I do kirtan in the Hindu tradition and zikr in the Sufi tradition. I intone Hebrew prayers and Latin hymns. I sing songs of praise to Mother Earth and Mother Mary, cry out in longing for the Beloved and invoke the presence of the Shekinah on Shabbat. I sing in my car, sing in the shower, sing to my grandchildren in utero and then continue long after they are born. I am no Billie Holiday, and I cannot sing opera. I would never audition for *American Idol*. But I can play "La Llorona" on the guitar and I know every word by heart. And when I sing in Spanish about that heartbroken ghost, my own heart breaks open wide.

The truth is, I am also a lover of quiet. When I am home alone, I rarely put on music. I require complete silence and solitude to write. If someone is listening to the news on the radio while we are having a conversation, I usually end up requesting that they turn it off. If you ask me a question while Amy Goodman is reporting on the occupation of the West Bank, I will be unable to formulate a response. There is a channel in my psyche for sound and another reserved for soundlessness. Both bring me closer to the divine.

Images

Look at art. Plant yourself in a comfortable chair with a cup of tea beside you and turn the pages of that coffee-table book you've been meaning to go through but never have (preferably while listening to music!). Stroll through a gallery in your hometown or make a point to visit a local art museum wherever you travel. Buy art. Not only does it support people who are offering beauty and meaning to a world obsessed by gadgets, but it sends a signal to your soul: art matters. Study Neolithic cave drawings and investigate the Black Madonnas of southern Europe. Familiarize yourself with the distinctions between impressionism and expressionism. Be as curious about political art as plein air.

And don't stop there! Make art. Stock up on watercolors and good paper, felt-tip markers and colored pencils. Spread them out on the kitchen table and, like a child, lose yourself in creative play (preferably while listening to music!). Build a kiln and dig your own clay. Turn a lawn into a labyrinth. Color in coloring books with your grandchildren. Color outside the lines. Learn to weave. Practice perspective. Sketch nudes. Please don't let that bossy little voice inside your head have its way. You do not have to be picked up by an elite Manhattan gallery to be worthy of creative self-expression. Something magical happens when you slow down enough to put brush to canvas, chisel to stone. Something mystical.

Try new things. Or don't. Consider kindling old things with the flame of your curiosity. Gather flowers from your garden as if each blossom were a blessing from the fairies, and then arrange them as an act of thanksgiving. Make your salads into mandalas. Reclaim your wardrobe as holy vestments and carry them with badass nobility. As you put on your makeup, imagine that you are, as my friend Lama Tsultrim Allione says of her deep red lipstick, "adorning the goddess." Place candles around your tub, drape a Kashmiri shawl over your office chair, prepare your morning tea as an offering to the universe.

My childhood home has been compared to a folk-art museum. Wherever my mother has traveled, mostly throughout the Americas, she has collected objects of beauty and installed them in her handmade house in the mountains of New Mexico. The house itself, crafted of wood and stone, adobe and glass, is a work of art. Paintings and sculptures, contemporary and ancient, adorn every nook and all the walls. It would take a lifetime to absorb the magical things nestled there. Each time I go home I discover something I had never really seen before. It's like a combination of a mythic fairy house and an avant-garde cultural exhibition. And it's not only the works of human hands my mother collects. She also grows dozens of varieties of plants. She collects flowers and arranges them in coiled vessels and slim bud vases. She picks and prunes and laces and fluffs them. This offers her the opportunity to encounter a new work of art every day.

Growing up with a mother who sees and creates beauty wherever she goes has planted in me a beauty lens I cannot remove. My mother never mentions God. She does not subscribe to an established belief in some perfect world to come. But more than any person I have known, she has awakened my perceptions to the endless miracles unfolding from the center of this world.

Remember: you do not need to look beyond what is already in your life to uncover a brimming basket of mystical inspiration. The distinction between spiritual books and not-spiritual books is a matter of whatever opens your heart and brings you closer to the divine at any given moment. Same with music: maybe Gregorian chants stir some kind of wordless yearning in you and tears spring to your eyes. But maybe it's a Stevie Wonder song that gives you the felt sense of something sublime. Living a creative life may not require anything other than mindfully strolling the stands at your local farmers' market and picking your favorite-colored vegetables and then preparing them with love for your family's dinner (preferably while listening to music!).

To be a mystic is to harvest the bounty of your own soul-garden. This is a space that is both wild and tended. It is ever-changing, and likely to surprise you. Sometimes it is fecund and lush, and other times it is arid. Do not be alarmed when the conditions of your soul seem to dry up. Explore the hidden life beneath the surface, and be patient. The rains will come again.

Translation Darshan

Translation is the most creative writing I have ever done. Nothing is more beautiful to me than taking a paragraph of thorny theology in sixteenth-century Castilian and rendering it into luminous and accessible twenty-first-century English. Translating the mystics makes me feel like a restorer of medieval tapestries. My job is to gather the masterpieces stashed for too long in the dusty halls of academia, unroll them and study them closely, then unravel the strands, dip them into vats of fresh dye, and reweave each piece, restoring them to their former glory.

But more than that, to translate the perennial wisdom of beings like the fourteenth-century English anchoress Julian of Norwich, the fiery Spanish saint Teresa of Avila and her protégé John of the Cross, is to take my seat in the presence of the awakened ones and be transfigured by the encounter. It is intimate, almost erotic. It is humbling. Like you, maybe, I haven't managed to entirely sidestep the voices of the patriarchy, and they sometimes whisper in my ear: *Who do you think you are? How dare you presume to speak for these enlightened beings? Why should anyone believe you have earned the right?* But I'm onto them now. I smile and nod and go back to work. Defeated, the disembodied bullies fade away.

It wasn't until I was in my late thirties at the end of the last millennium that I gave birth to my first book baby: a new translation of the mystical classic *Dark Night of the Soul*, by Saint John of the Cross. By that time, I had been on a serious spiritual path for a couple of decades. I had followed a few genuine spiritual teachers and a few more not-so-genuine ones. I knew about the reciprocal power of darshan in the Hindu tradition: when you behold a deity with an open heart, it beholds you back. When you approach the guru, either still living or no longer, the guru reaches for you. Or, as Allah so evocatively says in the Hadith Qudsi, "Take one step toward me, I will take ten steps toward you. Walk toward me, I will run toward you."

When I began translating John of the Cross, I quickly realized that I had plunged into this kind of mystical exchange. I crossed the threshold of my office as if I were bending to enter a cave in the Himalayas. I lit a candle, propped up my volume of John's collected works in Spanish on my left side and a fat Spanish dictionary on my right, and the centuries between us melted. I was bowing at the feet of the master. I was leaning in close to listen to every word he uttered. The air was charged with *shakti*—the dynamic, feminine energy coursing through every particle of creation, according to Hindu wisdom—and sometimes I became almost too intoxicated to work. I would have to take a deep breath, lure myself back to my body, and step lightly aside to let John have his way with me. I trusted him to use me to convey his essential teachings to a contemporary and global audience.

It worked. And so, I kept going, translating Teresa of Avila's autobiography, *The Book of My Life*, and her masterwork, *The Interior Castle*. I translated *The Showings* of Julian of Norwich from Middle English. In between, I wrote a few books of my own, but the truth is, I never could have dared to speak in my own voice if these beloved mystics had not been so generous as to share their voices with me.

I rarely admit this, but translating feels like channeling. I offer myself as the instrument for someone else's breath, their voice, their song. We labor together, with a blend of reckless joy and diamond precision. I am not only the masters' most ardent disciple; I am their personal assistant and faithful editor. I feel the same way

when I teach a class or lead a retreat. I have been stunned into silence often enough by the power of the mystics to say what they
want to say using my imperfect mouth that I have learned how to
shut up and let them do so.

Using the Mind to Transcend the Mind

Here is an ordinary mystical phenomenon for you: language can
be a rocket ship that blasts you into the cosmos, leaving words far
behind. This is why scripture study is essential in every religion
that has a compendium of texts. It is far more than an intellectual
activity. It is prayer itself.

In Judaism it takes the form of Torah study. Before we even
begin, we utter a prayer of thanksgiving for the Torah itself. Then
we dive in, reading a passage slowly, pondering it, closing our eyes
to digest it, talking about it with others. We embrace resonance and
we do not shy away from dissonance. We grapple and argue, win-
nowing out a truth that feels authentic and alive. The definition of
Torah can be broad. Although it often refers to the first five books
of the Hebrew Bible, what Christians call the Old Testament, it also
can refer to all the books of the Hebrew Bible, plus rabbinic writings, commentaries, and reflections. In this sense, Torah is a living
text, ever-unfolding. Whenever you offer your insights, you are
contributing to Torah yourself!

In the Hindu tradition, sacred study is part of the path of Jnana
Yoga. This is a practice that engages the mind to transcend the
mind. Through meditation and inquiry, we train our awareness to
stop identifying with fleeting thoughts and drop down to a place

of vibrant openness. We check our compulsion to regret the past and project into the future and practice being present with things as they are. We learn to see beyond our habitual ways of understanding the world and our place in it. Although this is a path that may appeal to the more philosophically inclined among us, anyone can pick up a mystical text and, like a Jnana yogi, give themselves over to the adventure of excavating the jewels nestled inside.

One of my favorite contemplative methods is a version of *Lectio Divina* ("sacred reading," in Latin) that I have adapted to jibe with my own artistic sensibilities. Traditionally, this Christian monastic practice (which must have sprouted from the garden of Torah study in Judaism, even if the fathers of monasticism were not aware of this) involved three stages: reading a passage of holy scripture, pondering something that jumps out for you, and then speaking to God about it. My technique is less structured. And I rarely use a biblical passage. I am more likely to pick a poem, one that may or may not be overtly "spiritual." I read it three times and feel no compulsion to run it by God. The first time I read a poem is like knocking on the poem's door. On the second reading, the door may open. And if I'm lucky, the third time I read it I walk into the landscape of the poem and it welcomes me home.

Melting into Music, Dissolving into Rivers

My friend Nancy is a mystic disguised as an atheist. For Nancy, the river canyons of the desert Southwest are sacred shrines, and music is worship. Her body has been a faithful companion, carrying her into and through the wild places of this earth. Her lips and lungs have worked with her to produce the most sublime sounds. Now, things are changing. Nancy's central nervous system is deteriorating. And her inner life, simultaneously a field of battle and a place of refuge, is lighting up.

1983

Snowmelt from the Rocky Mountains was gushing into the Colorado River as it flowed between the walls of the Grand Canyon. Trained as a classical flutist in her native New York, Nancy had joined a rafting expedition as their team musician. Her job was to play the flute as they floated on the current by day and sat around the campfire in the evenings.

Nancy's passion for the Southwest was fresh and all-encompassing. She had first gone to Taos to ski in the early 1970s, and then returned for a summer music festival a few years later and fell deeply in love with the Sangre de Cristo Mountains, the Rio Grande Gorge, and the cultural richness of northern New Mexico. She flew home to New York, packed her car, and drove back to Taos for good. She began to play improvisational music with different kinds of flutes, alone and in the company of other renegade artists. Finding herself cradled now like a tiny creature in the majestic lap of the Grand Canyon, her old friend Bach felt out of place. She stowed her silver flute and began playing the bamboo flute she had also brought along, creating music that spoke to her through the numinous landscape she was witnessing.

When the group pulled up on the sandy shore after a day on the water, Nancy would slip the bamboo flute into the back of her ball cap and scramble up the rocky embankments, exploring natural stone amphitheaters, ancient cliff dwellings and granaries. Perched above camp, she would play her simple flute, a spontaneous love song to the river and rocks, to the summer thunderheads and the swallows that darted in and out of holes in the sandstone cliffs. In rapture, Nancy would melt into the music, permeate the landscape, disappear into something larger and yet more intimate than she had ever experienced.

2017

Nancy and her husband, Vishu, take a solo canoe trip down the Green River in Utah. They meander through Labyrinth and Stillwater canyons, winding through Canyonlands National Park. Again, Nancy brings her wood flute and allows herself to become the instrument, just as the land had taught her thirty-five years earlier. Nancy keeps a journal.

> Brought to my knees once again by the utter perfection of canyon walls, and the challenge of walking this earth. Transcendent beauty, intractable physicality, struggle to feel my innate melding with nature while being humbled and halted again and again, hanging onto one of my most treasured and wordless connections, feeling the eternity of these rocks and the fragility of these bones.

Brought to her knees, yes. Halfway between that first river trip through the Grand Canyon and this adventure in Canyonlands, with many expeditions in between, Nancy was diagnosed with multiple sclerosis. Here on the Green River, she grapples with the progression of her disease, finding a connection that transcends her physical limitations. Losing it again.

> I sit here on my butt-dipped chair and take it in, melt into the shapes and colors, sights and sounds, sensations and serenity, and feel what connects me to my humanness. That is still there, although the Nancy spirit yearns to fly up these canyons, deeper into the heart of things, pressing against the rock, merging with the water, strong limbs carrying me along the wash and up the cliffs.

1983

As the group was getting ready for bed, Nancy quietly perched beside the river and, hidden from view, began to play an improvised lullaby. Stunned, the rafters looked up at the sky. Cascades of bamboo flute music poured over them. The power rising from the landscape flowed through Nancy's instrument and touched the people she was there to serve. It was a great circle of sacred song. Minutely personal and utterly transcendent. This was communion. She realized that this magic could not happen alone.

2017

No longer able to climb boulders, Nancy meanders along the sandy paths where she knows a multitude have passed in centuries gone by. She forgot to bring along reading material but she requires no distraction; she can't take her eyes off the water, the sky, the canyon walls.

> Layover day in Three Canyon. Couldn't bear to leave, even after considering early bailout at Mineral Bottom, following two bruising falls last night. But as so often happens, the "never do this again" becomes the most blissful moment ever—morning Native flute duet with the birds, "practicing" in the face of stunning rock walls, swimming in a perfect canyon pool without touching bottom. Afternoon spent in stillness, soporific well-being, true sense of ease and relaxation, feeling the air move over my body like soft silk—truly the best caress.

Nancy's aesthetic appreciation for the beauty of nature is giving way to a wordless immersion into the landscape. From her Green River Notes:

> The morning air is so perfect now that I have the sense of being embraced by it. Somehow my body (mind) has lost its separateness from the sky, sand, sage, and rocks.

2023

Nancy cannot climb snowy ridges and ski down them anymore. Navigating between her kitchen and bathroom requires every ounce of attention and fortitude now. She recently retired from a thirty-year career as the director of the chamber music group she founded, in which she also performed as a flutist throughout each season.

Her body is beginning to slowly dissolve back into the earth. She is watching this process with something like awe.

"I'm experiencing my own disappearance every day," Nancy tells me. "As the parts are taken away, I wonder what's left. It needs to be okay with me if the essence is gone and nothing replaces it." And sometimes it is okay. Sometimes it is definitely not. Once athletic and in charge of the way her body moved through space, now Nancy's gait is lurching and unstable. She falls in parking lots and concert halls, on her front porch as she steps out to glimpse the sunset through the piñon pines. She is taken to her knees again and again.

"Everyone is going to die," Nancy reminds me.

It's just that Nancy can see her own death happening slowly before her eyes.

"I'd like to be someone who can authentically embrace what's happened to me. I don't want to be consumed by resentment and regret." Melting into music taught Nancy to listen deeply. She wants to harness that capacity to hold the reality of her physical condition. "It's about showing up for whatever is happening. Not trying to make it better, but really being with it."

Forty years after her first expedition to the Grand Canyon, and unable to stay away from the deep river canyons she refers to as temples, Nancy and her husband recently took a guided raft trip down the San Juan River. As before, Nancy kept River Notes:

> I came down here to be different from my usual self, to reduce that which I think I need, to reconnect to that which I hold sacred, to know I can push myself from the self-perceived comfort of limitation and habit, and to

take that back for solace when I become a patient again. And sure enough the patterns of pain have dissipated.

Nancy harnessed the power of this brave journey to prepare for an upcoming medical procedure to slow the progress of her degenerative condition. She took the river with her to that hospital in New York. She brought canyons and crows, willows and tamarisks, silence and birdsong and flute music.

> I will carry this holy ground to the table where my own sweet stem cells will be injected into my spinal column, to heal this body that still wants to live, if only to return to the humbling and stunning stone and life-giving water.

This is the path of the ordinary mystic. Practicing to become an instrument through which the spirit of the universe makes her music. Entering the natural world as if it were a cathedral and praising with the whole of your heart, and your full body. Listening deeply for that one universal note that Nancy has been seeking all her life. And, when everything by which you once defined yourself is taken away, resting in that emptiness. Because art and love, mountains and canyons, have taught you how to dissolve into beauty, and dissolving feels like wholeness.

Practice

LECTIO DIVINA

Choose a passage from a sacred text, such as the *Dhammapada* or the Bible, or a poem by a classical or contemporary poet that may or may not be overtly "spiritual," and read it slowly (aloud or silently) three times, pausing to take a few mindful breaths in between, and allow the words to knock on the door of your heart, opening beyond themselves into a larger field of connection to the sacred.

※

WRITING PROMPT:

Ask a question of a sage and write
the answer in their voice.

FIVE

Connection

Building and Tending
Beloved Community

No One Can Save You

Have you been scanning the horizon for an enlightened being to come rescue humanity from the mess we've made? Someone with the perfect blend of spiritual insight and political savvy, who effortlessly sacrifices themselves for the rest of us? Someone who speaks well and looks good? If so, it's not your fault. You've been conditioned to expect this. Every spiritual tradition I know of promises some version of a savior, a redeemer, a second coming.

But stop it. Stop waiting for the lone prophet, the singular sage. Ours is a time of collective awakening, of reciprocity, of active participation in the web of interbeing. To find the mystical in the everyday is not a solo enterprise. It's not just about you enlarging your capacity for wonder, deepening your equanimity quotient, and brushing up your relationship with a higher power. Give up the never-ending self-improvement project. It's futile and beside the point. We need each other. We belong to each other. We stretch and grow each other. Sometimes you are the seeker, sometimes the teacher. Each of us has something essential to contribute, inextricably bound with our individual quirks and gifts. Quit dividing up the world into those who have the magical qualities to fix what is broken and the rest of us, all the broken ones. The servants and the served are one glorious, messy human family, of which you are a beloved member. One who sometimes has her shit together and can patch the leaky roof and sometimes needs to go to bed with a hot water bottle.

Find your people. What Ram Dass called your "soul pod." And if you can't find it, build it. Tend it with all your heart. Then, community becomes a path of healing, homecoming, and happiness—even if it doesn't look like your idea of the grouping of souls you would have arranged had you been in charge of the universe. If you cannot see the face of the divine in the elderly lady who sings too loud at church or in your best friend's introverted new boyfriend, you are not likely to find it anywhere. Maybe it's time to renew your vows to beloved community.

Let Your Saints Fuck Up

With her dark beauty and charisma, the sixteenth-century mystic Teresa of Avila spent the first half of her life manipulating every man she encountered and the second half trying to resist the impulse to do so. Three hundred years later the French nun Thérèse of Lisieux, who started begging God at a young age to turn her into a saint, hated herself for hating the way the sister beside her in the refectory chewed her food. Siddhartha Gautama, aka the Buddha, abandoned his wife and child to pursue his own enlightenment. Even Lord Ram, incarnation of God in the Hindu tradition, couldn't bear the thought that his wife Sita had cheated on him with the ten-headed demon who abducted her and, after arranging her epic rescue, insisted that she walk through fire to prove her purity.

Our spiritual heroes were not always nice. They didn't always behave in the ways we associate with sanctity, and were even known to willfully misbehave. They were sometimes petty and grumpy, they binged on salty snacks and drank too much sake, they could be self-involved or easily offended. Just. Like. You.

Please don't be disappointed. This is not a problem. It's great news! It means that if these mythic mystics could fuck up—if they could blurt out inane and inappropriate things at dinner parties and stop speaking to their mothers for months at a time—then you can forgive yourself for all the ways you participate in the human predicament. What is interesting about the Hildegard of Bingens and Rumis, the Prophet Muhammads and Mother Marys, is not the way they match up with some exalted image of holiness but rather that they were ordinary extraordinary beings. Their quirks and faults are entwined with their gifts. We do not turn to them despite their shadows; we appreciate them because they were human beings doing their best to love unconditionally, to give of themselves extravagantly, to forgive their neighbors and themselves again and again. Just. Like. You.

We are set up to revere Buddhist monks from Japan and Catholic humanitarians from India, and then, when they act like human beings, we are offended. Spiritual genius and bad behavior are not mutually exclusive. The Reverend Doctor Martin Luther King Jr. probably picked fights with his wife when he was tired and hungry. Maybe Mother Teresa of Calcutta held religious views you consider draconian. Does this mean that we should dump these iconic wisdom keepers in search of more reliable role models? Au contraire! False holiness is a red herring that takes us away from the complex and luminous center of things. Everything we need to learn about how to show up for this fleeting incarnation with our hearts open and our sleeves rolled up is available to us when we look to the journals of the wild Jewish feminist Etty Hillesum, for instance, who, though plagued by neuroses and prone to partying, intentionally accompanied her people to their deaths in a concentration camp when she could have wriggled out of it. When we hear the legend of how Shiva cut off his own son's head when the boy was guarding his mother so that she could bathe in peace, and then stuck an elephant's head on his shoulders to appease his stricken wife, we see that even the gods can be impulsive and absurd.

The invitation is to see our teachers as human beings striving to make the best of their humanity, trying—and sometimes failing—to extend themselves for the greater good. Let's love them not despite their flaws but rather because of them! Can you allow your heart to grow tender in the light of their imperfections? Let's climb up the scaffolding we built with our own hands and carry our heroes back down to earth where they belong.

I am the most unexceptional person I know. My IQ is average, I can be alternately judgmental and insecure, sometimes shifting within seconds, and I get so frustrated with electronics I want to throw my computer through the window just to hear the glass shatter. I'm mortified by my nose and chin in profile, and I despair over my cellulite. Do I need to keep going? I think you understand. I'm just like you. Just as ordinary. No more or less flawed or enlightened than anyone else.

Which is why it bewilders me when I meet people who look at me with stars in their eyes. I can see that they are not seeing me; they are seeing the stars in their eyes. They think that because I write books about women's wisdom, I must be a wise woman. This is an understandable mistake, but it is a mistake. I am doing the best I can to walk through this world doing as little damage as possible and sharing as much lovingkindness as I can, just like the people who mistake me for someone special. Sometimes at big gatherings people approach me with trepidation, as if they are afraid I will yell at them or tell them to get lost. I look around, trying to figure out who they're searching for, and when I realize it's me, I have to fight the urge to burst out laughing. If only they knew! They are often in a big rush to tell me something important about themselves, usually having to do with a great loss or a life-changing spiritual experience, as if my bearing witness for those few minutes will give the restless butterfly of their souls a safe spot to alight at last. I wish I could be that leafy branch. I wish I could offer a soft place to land. But by exalting me they've made me inaccessible.

Also, I'm afraid of heights. I think one of the reasons it makes me so uncomfortable when people elevate me is that I know from experience I am sure to disappoint them and come tumbling down from that pedestal and shatter. Which hurts. The minute I detect someone pinning their spiritual hopes on me, I get nervous. I have left a wake of disillusioned followers behind me, and it breaks my heart. I am not interested in perpetuating hierarchical models that single out anyone as more spiritually evolved than anyone else. I do not want disciples. I want companions.

Soul Friends

Like a honeybee gathering pollen, seek your soul family. They often appear in disguise. Their manners may be questionable. Their religious beliefs may diverge from your own, their first language may not be yours, their skin color might grant them privileges you don't have access to, or maybe their ancestors were persecuted by yours. They love people you don't even like. Perhaps they don't bathe often enough for your tastes, or they wear perfume that reminds you of something decomposing in the rosebushes. Look past these details. Trust the sense of homecoming you feel in their presence.

Your soul companions could be your best friends from childhood who still call on your birthday, or on the anniversary of your child's death, or from pre-op before being wheeled in for a lumpectomy, or after listening to a podcast while driving south to Los Angeles from San Francisco that reminds them of you. Or they could be the shy young man you met in tango class who transforms into a supernova on the dance floor. A co-worker who reads Emily

Dickinson poems on their lunch break. Your twelve-year-old granddaughter. They may be on a spiritual path, passionate about attaining union with God, or they may find God-talk ludicrous, even dangerous. Acclaimed or obscure, healthy or ailing, elderly or new to this earth, your soul friends are the magic sprinkled over your ordinary mystical life.

In the Upaddha Sutta, Buddha says, "admirable friendship, admirable companionship, admirable camaraderie is the whole of the holy life." He called friendship a jewel, named it *sangha*, and invited us to take refuge there. In Celtic wisdom, a soul friend is known as an *anam cara*. Your *anam cara* is someone who makes the effort to see beyond your masks and not turn away, someone who reciprocates by taking the risk to let you truly see them. In his contemplative masterpiece *No Man Is an Island* the great twentieth-century sage Thomas Merton points out that our human weaknesses play a vital role in our lives, that we are all deficient in different ways, and that when we come together, we create wholeness. This vision of interdependence is at the heart of Buddhism and Judaism, of environmental science and quantum theory. We do, as it turns out, complete each other. In the presence of our soul friends, we are safe to explore our shadow, knowing we belong to each other, that our flaws link us up with the rest of the flawed human family.

I have an unlikely yet irreplaceable assortment of soul friends. Catholic priests and Buddhist monks, corporate executives and academics, artists and activists. Some are elders, others teenagers. They are cisgendered and transgendered. My soul friends do not even have to be alive. Saint Teresa of Avila is my soul friend. So is my namesake, the South Asian poet Mirabai. They can be mythic beings, like Tara, the Tibetan bodhisattva of compassion, and the Shekinah, the indwelling feminine presence of God in my ancestral Judaism.

Some of my soul friends are animals. My mixed-up mutt Lola, for example, who ricocheted off the furniture when she first came to live with us and still bursts with joy upon seeing us again each morning. And Ruby, my enormous Labradoodle, who always seems to know when my heart is troubled and whose gaze reminds me of a wise and kindly gorilla. The magpies and ravens who live in the poplar trees that border our property are my soul friends. I think they know my name. They greet me when I step outside, and I call back to them. I feel connected to the unseen creatures on my hikes who I know are living vibrant lives all around me, from the coyotes and elk to the rabbits and voles, from the prickly pear cactus to the mycelium. Current studies of nonhuman life-forms are confirming what Indigenous peoples have always known (and our own intuition confirms): animals have consciousness; plants are aware; mountains and rivers and storms are sentient; subatomic particles know what they're doing. The land and the sky, the ocean and the moon, behold us back.

There may be seasons to our soul friendships. Some endure for a lifetime, yet others flare up and fizzle out. I have had deep friends, people who have witnessed my most profound life challenges, whose love and wisdom have changed me, with whom I have lost all contact. I think of them wistfully, but feel no need to rekindle our connection. It is done. There are people whose presence in my life once felt as vital as water, but who betrayed me in some fundamental way that compelled me, despite my preferences otherwise, to let them go.

After years of friendship, during which I spilled my most vulnerable secrets, one beloved woman (indoctrinated, it must be noted, by a highly patriarchal religious paradigm) felt compelled to write me a letter recounting every incident in which she had found my behavior disappointing, and enumerating all my perceived faults and transgressions in brutal detail, making it clear that if I did not address each one with humility and a sincere desire to change, she could no longer be in relationship with me. She used the very things I had confided in her as weapons against me. I'm all for constructive criticism, but it's a lot easier to take it in when it's delivered with love. Mary Poppins had it right: a spoonful of sugar helps the medicine go down. After reading this woman's diatribe, I felt like I had been poisoned. Like I had been beaten by bandits and thrown in the river. And worse, like I deserved it. It took me many months (and the support of other soul friends) to recover. A soul friend helps you see the places where you could grow and flourish, yes, but if they make you feel like shit, it may be a sign that the relationship has run its course.

A soul friend is someone with whom you can take a walk in companionable silence, but also with whom you can't shut up. Inspired and inspiring conversation comes pouring out, your separate contributions mingling in the air between you and creating a much bigger reality than either of you could access without the other. The topic may not be overtly spiritual in nature, but it has the effect of uplifting you both. Maybe you're discussing the refugee crisis at the US border and how an Iranian immigrant you know goes down to Tijuana to dance with migrant children from Mexico. Or sustainable fashion trends, or the dangers of artificial intelligence, or your daughter's divorce. The intimacy is deep and it is holy. The words are like flames; they ignite you and warm you. Between the words something wordless shimmers, something that soothes old wounds and renews your faith in this perilous world.

My friend Bill is a Catholic priest and an iconographer. On the surface, we have little in common. Yet we play essential parts in each other's lives. When my daughter Jenny died, Bill blessed her body, and when my granddaughter Naya was born, he blessed her birth. When Bill had a cardiac event and we did not know whether he would ever wake from a coma, my own heart shattered and I didn't think I would be able to recover from his death. When he did survive, a new fervor entered our relationship, as if every conversation might be our last. We do talk about God. We talk about God a lot. God is our code word for everything that is wondrous and mysterious and hidden at the heart of our deepest heartache and most childlike delight. He teaches me about saints I've never heard of. When I see Bill's name light up my phone, I stop whatever I'm doing and pull up a chair. I know it's going to be a long visit, and that if I let myself be distracted by multitasking, I will miss something. Something sacred.

Same with my friend Andrew, a British scholar of the mystics who has studied and practiced the world's wisdom traditions more deeply and with greater passion than anyone I have ever known. Andrew is a prophet. He shouts from the rooftops, exhorting us all to wake up from our trance of capitalistic complacency and do whatever we can to save the burning world. He used to be so strident that he alienated half the people who dared to listen. He had opinions on everything from the global threat of authoritarianism to where his friends might consider donating their expendable income. Over the years, mellowed by heartbreak, illness, and a genuine willingness to face up to his own darkness, Andrew has become luminously kind. He has a gift for seeing into people's souls and lifting their unique gifts into the light. He lifts mine. I take notes when Andrew talks. He inevitably has just the right insight for my new writing project, blessings for my marriage, recommendations for books and music that shift my consciousness and transfigure my heart. I cannot imagine a world without Andrew in it.

Bill and Andrew are just a couple of a host of soul companions. They seem to love me unconditionally, and I love them so hard it hurts. Would I have purposely paired myself up with either of them? Probably not. They are both queer white men with solid religious convictions. They have access to privileges I do not and have experienced homophobia I have not. And yet they wound their way into my life and laid down roots. Our conversations are intoxicating and curative. It is a relief to be able to talk about our souls and the soul of the world without apology. These men speak my spirit's mother tongue. I am grateful to the universe for sending them to me.

And then there is Willow. A towering tree of joy. A gentle mountain. Both serene and incandescent. Young enough to be my daughter, with wisdom far beyond her age. How did Willow learn so much so soon? She has a gift, yes. She is exceptionally intelligent, true. But she has harnessed that intellectual capacity and hitched it to the horse of heartbreak. Willow has experienced abandonment and betrayal no young girl should ever have to endure (and which, tragically, many do). She stood in that wind as it buffeted her, and, like the tree she is named for, she bent and did not break. By the time we met, Willow had integrated her losses into the vast tapestry of her soul and emerged with a sense of childlike wonder that infuses the most ordinary moments with luminosity. Making a salad, watching the moon rise, singing harmonies.

Willow started off as my assistant and quickly became my creative partner. She keeps all the gears of my vocation turning in harmony. She is my personal DJ, creating the perfect playlists for every occasion, from a writing retreat to a road trip. She helps me say no when my impulse is to say yes and then wish like hell I hadn't. Willow has read nearly every word I've written and gets me more completely than anyone ever has. And her shadow matches up with mine. There is a mother-shaped hole in Willow's heart and a daughter-shaped hole in mine. The deaths of my daughter and of Willow's mother transfigured the landscape of our lives. It would be easy for our two wounds to meld in unconscious and unhealthy ways. And so, right from the beginning, we named this. We walk with care through each other's lives. There is ample space between us; we give each other the gift of autonomy. We are caring without being cloying, available without being intrusive, honest while staying kind. Willow has reeducated me to center my life in joy, and her quiet sorrow has taught me how to mourn.

There are many other soul friends I could tell you about. Some would be surprised to hear themselves mentioned, either because I have not conveyed how much they mean to me, or because they may not have considered our connection to be "spiritual." Others might wonder why I have not included them in this little list, remembering the times we have wept together, built things together, traveled and taught and written together. The truth is, the older I grow and the more people I lose, the deeper every relationship carves itself into me and the more everyone I meet becomes a soul friend. To live as ordinary mystics is to reclaim the people and tasks of everyday life as imbued with grandeur. Or at least, unutterable tenderness.

Mentors

Soul relationships are not always horizontal. Sometimes your teachers are soul friends, or your doctors, or your dad. There may be a power differential. They might be older than you are, or more famous, or have skills to which you are aspiring. Some of my deepest soul friends are my mentors.

Natalie Goldberg, for instance. Natalie has been in my life since 1973 when I had just turned twelve and she was hired as the creative writing teacher at our alternative school in Taos. A dozen ragamuffin kids gathered around her every day, sitting on old kilims that covered the dirt floor of our hand-built hogan, taking turns stoking the fire in the woodstove, while Natalie read to us from the haiku of Basho and *The Ballad of the Sad Café* by Carson McCullers. She handed out spiral-bound notebooks in an array of bright colors, assigned us writing prompts like "an unforgettable meal" and "the last time I saw my grandmother" and let us write whatever we felt like. Just like Naomi Tatarsky, who founded our school and had always encouraged us to write "stream of consciousness," Natalie didn't care about punctuation. Or spelling! There was nothing we were not allowed to say, and the only way we could fail was by failing to be real.

My connection with my mentor did not end with that first year in Taos. Natalie went on to develop writing as a spiritual practice and has transformed millions of lives besides mine. Yet we have maintained a close personal bond, and she feels more like family to me than a teacher. Natalie has always encouraged me to risk everything to be a writer. Approval, convenience, a stable home life. She has taught me to be my own robust advocate in the publishing business, and she has warned me that other women may find it easier to support my sorrows than my successes. I do not always agree with Natalie (who is surprised when I point out that she can be a teensy bit bossy), but I never doubt her wisdom or her love. She can be blunt to the point of shocking, doting to excess, as still as a mountain or bursting with childlike joy in the face of the most ordinary phenomena (dahlias in a cup, a flourless chocolate torte, a poem about a frayed sweater).

For the first couple of decades, I resisted Natalie's mentorship. It felt like she had me frozen as a troubled twelve-year-old hippie kid ("You always had this look of consternation on your face," she told me recently). I wanted her to acknowledge my progress as a street-smart meditation practitioner in my teens, an adoptive mother to abused children in my late twenties, a real writer once I had my first piece published in *The Sun* magazine in my thirties, and a bona fide author when my translations of the Christian mystics came out. And she did. Sort of. But I was always her little Paula (my name until I was fifteen), and I always will be.

And you know what? I have come to appreciate it. I love being Natalie's darling protégé. I love when she brags about me to her friends and students. I cherish having a woman in my life who has been here for every major passage: death, divorce, public accolade, and private anguish. My mentor's insights and sensibilities are so tightly woven with my own at this point I could not tease them apart if I tried. And I don't want to. I feel lucky to be entwined with Natalie Goldberg.

Over time, the gulf between our social locations grew smaller. Natalie began to recognize that I wasn't always needing something from her, that I also had something to give. A listening heart when she was grieving. Someone to complain to about changes in the publishing business, who knows through experience what she's up against. I was also a worthy hiking buddy, a restaurant recommender, a fellow dismantler of oppressive systems in the politics of American spirituality.

The other constant in my life has been Charlene. Unless you are a Buddhist scholar, or a researcher in the field of juvenile diabetes, or were a student of philosophy at the University of New Mexico in the 1980s, you have probably never heard of Charlene McDermott. That's not an accident. This is a woman who has spent her life cultivating the true self and has wasted very little energy accumulating worldly recognition.

Charlene was my graduate advisor when I was working on my master's degree in philosophy in my early twenties. Her background was in mysticism and epistemology, a perfect fit for my thesis, "The Paradox of the Expression of the Ineffable in Saint John of the Cross." I was fascinated by the pervasive phenomenon in which the mystics of all spiritual traditions and both genders claim that the mystical experience transcends all concepts and defies language, and yet they cannot seem to help themselves from offering a treasure trove of passionate poetry and sublime prose. It pours out of them in the wake of their experience of union with the divine.

Charlene had a special affinity for the Christian mystics, and she was the first person to alleviate my allergy to Christianity. I took all her classes and savored every word that emerged from her big red Italian lips (her Irish last name, an artifact of the first of her four marriages, concealed her Sicilian heritage). Our admiration was mutual. I could tell that, even though my intelligence quotient was nothing to brag about, I was one of those students who lights up in the face of the beauty of ideas and makes a professor feel like what she does matters. Charlene had attended an Ivy League college at age fifteen and had a couple of PhDs by the time she was my age (twenty-two). I, on the other hand, had an entirely alternative education, dropped out of high school and earned a GED, and struggled my way through a bachelor's degree in anthropology (with a concentration in archaeology) before staggering into graduate school in philosophy.

My colorful background did not earn me special treatment, however. My beloved mentor was uncompromising. She had me rewrite my thesis not once, not twice, but three times. This was no Natalie Goldberg, encouraging (and indulging) my "wild mind." Charlene insisted on rigorous scholarship, precise writing, and original thinking. I ended up being the first woman in our department to graduate "with distinction." I concluded that it was because the academy didn't know what to do with my unorthodox writing style (bordering on the ecstatic). But I also understood that it was because Charlene McDermott kicked my scholarly ass, and I was better for it. It didn't even hurt that much, because I knew my mentor not only believed in me, but loved me.

In her eighties now, Charlene is still my hero. An adoptive mother of two children herself, she inspired me to adopt my own daughters, and she agreed to be their godmother. When Jenny died, Charlene rushed to my side. When Jeff and I decided to get married (after five years of living together and raising two children and then losing one), it was Charlene we asked to officiate our wedding. She tracks my work in the world and checks in to make sure I'm eating. She shares just enough of her own struggles to remind me that she is human, and to give me the opportunity to love her back. I hear Charlene's quirky jokes coming out of my mouth and try to remember to embody her unique balance of intellectual rigor and lovingkindness.

When roles naturally fall away, souls take over. I will always cherish these two women as lifelong mentors. And it's a relief to walk side by side now, to look out on the world together and say, "Wow, did you see that?" And then to whistle in shared astonishment.

TLC List

I started a TLC list in my head and managed to keep it there for years. That collection of people in my life who are in some degree of crisis and could use a little love note to ease their burden. The ever-rotating hot spots calling for the water of my attention: a childhood friend, an avid mountain biker, who crashed her bike on her way to a catering gig and fractured her back and now is learning to walk again; a young father diagnosed with colon cancer and buckling under the weight of chemotherapy; a grieving widow, a child with a broken leg, my agent who retired, my faraway grandson who's learning to be a tattoo artist.

But the mind is unruly, and inevitably people I love would fall out of the list and get left behind. I would feel terrible when I remembered. Which would usually be when I was in the shower or about to step into a meeting, and so I'd stash them in a corner where they would get lost all over again. I was living in a constant state of low-level guilt and free-floating anxiety about all the loved ones I was neglecting. I switched to jotting them down on the to-do list I keep on my desk, but they often got buried amid reminders to call the plumber or introduce so-and-so to what's-his-name. Now I have a list on my phone, and when I've made the call or sent the text or email or occasionally a card, I tap the little bubble and the name disappears. I utter a prayer as it goes.

I don't fool myself into believing that my encouraging messages are going to alleviate their troubles. Tumors rarely go away overnight. Rehab is usually a step on a long journey up a tall mountain. A breakup breaks our hearts again and again. The ones we love will always need our tender loving care. We do the best we can. Sometimes a little loving does big work.

Your TLC list doesn't have to be a formal one. You can simply cultivate a stance of gentle vigil, your mystical antennae tuned to the presence of distress in the people around you. Keep dippers of heart-water handy, and when you have the chance, offer them. Try to leave the guilt behind. You bear burdens of your own. You get distracted. That's okay. When you look up again, there they will be: your friend's beloved stepmother home from the hospital after a severe case of pneumonia; a poet whose wife left her in the midst of a collaborative book project; a soul-sister freaking out about turning fifty. A little message from you can help them see God in the heart of the catastrophe.

Barrios and Bakeries

My friend Greg Boyle has buried 258 kids and counting. Founder of the world's largest and most successful gang intervention and rehabilitation program, Father G bears daily witness to the deepest shadows of the human condition.[1] He also offers a way out of the hopelessness and despair of intergenerational violence and into a circle of kinship and connection. Like flowering plants in a desert, the homies, as Father G fondly calls them, flourish when they come into contact with this unexpected, seemingly unearned, and extravagantly unconditional love. But sometimes they don't make it. They shoot each other. They go back to prison. They get shot and leave their mothers bereft, their siblings abandoned, their communities shattered.

---

1   See Homeboy Industries, https://homeboyindustries.org/: "For over 30 years, we have stood as a beacon of hope in Los Angeles to provide training and support to formerly gang-involved and previously incarcerated people, allowing them to redirect their lives and become contributing members of our community."

How does Father G endure such huge suffering? By disarming his heart, again and again. By believing against all odds in the power and radiance of love to outshine the ignorance of Otherizing. By refusing to affirm a god that is both tame and unapproachable, saying yes instead to a God who is wild and warm. Father G is the least preachy priest I have ever known (and I know plenty of radically inclusive clergy). His way of speaking is down-to-earth and accessible. When I point out how refreshing this is, how free of orthodoxy and evangelism, he shrugs and says, "Old tired dogmatic religious language blocks the pores of our souls and spirit, so it's best not to use it." This is what I mean by ordinary mysticism. A willingness to forgo prescribed belief systems that confine the great mystery to tidy categories that justify all manner of exclusionary behaviors. Starting from zero again and again, welcoming unknowingness, cultivating radical hospitality and unmitigated tenderness even when they are not reciprocated. Because this is where you have detected the fragrance of the sacred, within the fiery heart of the human predicament.

"God doesn't have a range of responses," Greg recently reminded me. "*I like this, I don't like that*. It is a singular response: *I will carry you, no matter what*." He went on to say that we must bring that warmheartedness into how we are with each other. "Carry the wildness of welcome and hospitality. Erase lines, dismantle the barriers that exclude." The motto of Homeboy Industries, the organization Greg founded in Los Angeles, sums it all up: *There is no us and them; there is only us*.

The homies have taught Greg everything worth knowing. A homegirl once told him that love is now the lens through which she looks at the world, and he has tried to maintain that perspective every day since, and to help the rest of us cultivate it. "I'm used to being watched," one homeboy admitted. "But I'm not used to being seen." Being beheld through a loving gaze is transformative. It is scary, but not as scary as wondering whether a rival gang member is going to drive by your house and open fire, and whether your baby daughter will become collateral damage.

"God is love, yes," Greg tells me. "But that's not so much about *how* God is as *where* God is. It's geographical. God lives in the loving. The more you love, the more it is amplified. Love never stops loving. You want to be where love is. That is the mystical life."

And the homies are a bunch of mystics. "I'm going to love you even if you tell me to fuck off," one homie said to a former rival as they worked side by side in Homeboy Bakery, the highly successful industry Greg and his team developed decades ago to lure gang members off the streets, to replace selling heroin with baking bread. Little by little, they learn each other's real names, and the names of their moms, and their favorite music, and their plans to earn their GEDs and remove the tattoos that signal their gang affiliation and trigger hatred and violence.

Many years ago, Greg's beloved colleague Rita died. She was a longtime organizer at Dolores Mission, the church where Greg had been a pastor throughout his early years in Boyle Heights. It was the poorest parish in Los Angeles, set in the middle of the two housing projects with the highest concentration of gangs in the city. Greg officiated Rita's funeral. That night he went to bed with a heart weighed down by sorrow. And he had a dream. Rita appeared to him and said, "All of us are born, all of us will die, and all we have left is the tender time in between."

The message couldn't have been clearer, a potent elixir distilled to its essence. This is the potion Greg drinks every day and offers to everyone he meets. Even me. When I finally met the radically loving priest a few years ago, we had already read each other's books and knew we had an affinity, but truly I could have been anybody, and he would have welcomed me as if I were a long-lost sister. He makes everyone feel cherished. He laughs at our jokes and asks about our kids and jots down any morsel of original wisdom we might acciden-tally utter and then quotes us later. Although incredibly busy and in demand, Greg invited me in for a luxurious conversation about the Spanish mystics and walking an interspiritual path. Our connection felt both ecstatic and comfortable. Greg Boyle dismantles my false models of what a saint is supposed to look like, how they might talk, where they should live. When he tells stories of the homies, his eyes fill with tears and he has to take off his glasses and wipe his face. His humility is his superpower.

Not everyone can dedicate their lives to being available to the poorest of the poor and the most damaged of the broken. But all of us can reclaim loving kinship as the thing that matters most, the only rudder that can steer our lives through these tumultuous waters, the most robust vessel in which to carry each other home.

Everybody's Lady

Maybe it happened. Maybe it didn't. But the legend itself changed everything, and the changes continue to ripple five centuries later.

We are told that Mother Mary appeared on a hill above Mexico City in 1531 and healed the shattered heart of a conquered people. They call her Nuestra Señora de Guadalupe, Our Lady of Guadalupe. Over the centuries, she has become everybody's lady. Not only folks from Mexico, not only Catholics. Both the privileged and the poor. The Guatemalan immigrant and the gynecologist from Salt Lake City. The true believer and the mostly unbeliever. Images of Nuestra Señora abound in hair salons and hospitals, on the altars of pagan priestesses and in corporate cubicles. I myself have at least half a dozen statues and framed prints of Nuestra Señora in my little house.

See if you can find yourself in this story.

One December day, ten years after the Spanish had overthrown the Aztec Empire of Tenochtitlan and replaced it with an empire of their own, an Indigenous farmer known as Juan Diego was heading down to the valley from his home in the mountains. Maybe he was going to church in the city, or maybe he was visiting the shrine of Tonantzin, the ancient Mother Goddess of his people. As he approached the Hill of Tepeyac, he heard the music of dozens of songbirds and wondered whether he had wandered into the Other World. At that moment, a beautiful woman appeared, hovering above the ground, supported by a crescent moon, encircled by rays of light.

"I am your compassionate mother," she spoke in Nahuatl, Juan Diego's own tongue, "and the mother of all."

Her skin was the dark brown of the Native people, her facial structure European. Her belly was rounded and she wore a traditional maternity belt, tied with the four-petaled flower of fertility.

The stars of her turquoise-tinted mantle reflected the exact position of the constellations during the winter solstice. Her rose-hued dress was the color of dawn, and new life seemed to flow from her tender gaze.

"I have chosen you, my beloved child," she said, "to go to the palace of the bishop and tell him I have a great desire that he build me a chapel here on this hill where I will listen to the lamentations of all who love me and I will remedy their miseries, afflictions, and sorrows." She instructed the peasant to inform the religious authorities that the Ever-Immaculate Mother Mary sent him.

This is where Juan Diego takes his place in the lineage of Reluctant Prophets that spans the ages and transcends religious affiliation. An impoverished Aztec peasant carrying the demands of a heavenly apparition to the highest echelons of imperialist society? Young Mother Mary herself resisted the annunciation. Who was she, a pregnant, unmarried Jewish teenager living under the tyranny of Roman rule, to bear the Messiah in her own womb? And then there was the Prophet Muhammad, an illiterate camel driver, who was meditating in a cave when the same angel Gabriel who appeared to Mary appeared to him and commanded him to memorize everything he said and "recite" it to all people, sowing the seeds that flowered into the Qur'an. When the Holy One appeared to Moses in the burning bush, Moses tried to use his speech impediment as an excuse to avoid returning to the palace of Pharaoh, who had threatened to kill him, and demanding that he let every single Jewish slave walk out of Egypt and make their way to Canaan in peace.

Saint after saint, mystic upon mystic, received visions and heard voices that bossed them around and upended their comfortable lives. Hildegard of Bingen and Sor Juana Inés de la Cruz, Rumi and Dogen, Dr. Martin Luther King Jr. and Dorothy Day. Not one of them bounced in their seats, shooting their hands in the air and crying out, "Pick me, God!"

But down to the city Juan Diego went. He knocked at the palace gates and waited a long, long time before Bishop Zumárraga condescended to see him. You can imagine how that went. The religious dignitary dismissed the corn-grower, who returned to Tepeyac Hill discouraged. He was pretty sure Our Lady had picked the wrong emissary, and when she appeared again, he told her so, suggesting she select someone with the power to get the job done.

But the beautiful Mother was not having it. She consoled Juan Diego, telling him to try again, making sure the bishop realized it was the Virgin Mary Herself who had sent him. The second time, the bishop cocked his head as Juan Diego described the magical woman clothed with the sun, standing on the moon, and seemed to consider the possibility that this might be real.

"I need a sign," Zumárraga blustered.

So, Juan Diego trudged back home to ponder his options. The next day he received word that his beloved uncle Juan Bernadino was dying and that he needed to go find a priest to administer last rites. Torn between duty to his family and devotion to the embodiment of Love itself, Juan Diego decided to take an alternate route to evade Our Lady altogether. No sooner had he circumvented Tepeyac Hill than she appeared anyway, assuring him that his uncle was not going to die after all, that she herself had already cured him.

Moreover, she knew exactly what she was doing when she chose Juan Diego as her mouthpiece.

"Hear me and understand well, my little son," Our Lady said. "Let nothing frighten or grieve you. Do not let your heart be disturbed." And then she spoke some of the most beloved words in the history of Marian apparitions: "Am I not here, I, who am your mother?"

This time, she sent him up to the top of the mountain, where she told him he would find a meadow blanketed with wild roses. He was to pick all the flowers he could, gather them into his cloak, and take them to the bishop. Since it was midwinter in the mountains and nothing was growing, the bishop would recognize this as a sacred sign, and he would agree to build her shrine. When Juan Diego crested the ridge and discovered the miraculous field just as she had described, Our Lady showed up and arranged the flowers herself, tucking them into the ayate fibers of his tilma, or cloak. Juan Diego sprinted back to the city and burst through the gates of the palace. As the Spanish bishop and his minions surrounded the Indigenous prophet, he opened his tilma, and in place of the wildflowers he had gathered, a cascade of Castilian red roses that grew only in Zumárraga's homeland fell at his feet. And if that were not astonishing enough, imprinted inside Juan Diego's cloak was the perfect image of the Virgin Mary, exactly as Juan had described her.

The bishop built her a chapel. And he constructed adjoining living quarters for Juan Diego, appointing him the task of safeguarding the miraculous tilma and tending the shrine to Our Lady. Over the centuries, this sacred spot, and the basilica eventually built there, has become a pilgrimage destination for millions—the heart-sick and the terminally ill, those who stagger under the weight of poverty and oppression, mothers whose sons have been lost to addiction, fatherless daughters, lovers who have been left, and those who fear they will never be loved. She receives them all, small brown Mary, beaming from her gilded frame, infusing them with the fragrance of the comfort she promised.

I went once. I, a middle-aged Jewish woman from a progressive community in the United States. I, who have a devotion to a Hindu guru and a dedicated Buddhist meditation practice. I, who dance with Sufis and pray with pagans. I, who half the time do not even believe in a personified god and the other half of the time long for union with God. She welcomed me, and I felt it. I felt it in every cell of my postmodern, transreligious being. I lit a candle for her and gave thanks for all the ways she has been with me in my darkest despair.

I notice she is with my friends, too. With Jenny, a refugee from Middle America, who built her own house out of recycled bottles and mud in the high desert of New Mexico, who writes songs and sings them through tears. For Aracely, an evangelical Christian from Chihuahua who cleans my house once a month and claims not to believe in Mary and the saints, yet when I bring up Guadalupe, she enkindles, and the stories pour out of her like sweet smoke. For my daughters, raised in ashrams, who keep her statue by their beds and invoke her during childbirth. She is the Mother of the Mestizo people, yes. She is the Goddess of the Americas. She is venerated by Catholics at the highest level. And she is everybody's Lady.

Am I not here, I, who am your Mother?

I have to believe she means me, too. And you. She means all of us. She leaves no one behind.

This does not entitle privileged white folks from the United States, like me, to blithely appropriate her, however. Anytime we hear the resounding call of a wisdom being from another culture and have the sincere desire to weave them into the tapestry of our spiritual lives, it comes with the responsibility to humbly acknowledge the source. Study it, name it, give gratitude. I love Mexico, but I am not a Mexicana. I resonate with Christian mysticism, but I am not Catholic. My heart says yes to the Earth Goddess, yet I am not Indigenous. If we help ourselves to the treasures of other cultures and religious traditions without reverence and tribute, we are committing acts of neocolonialism disguised as spirituality.

I must admit, my Latinx friends seem less concerned about this than I am. When I was on a book tour in Mexico City for the Spanish translation of *Wild Mercy*, my hosts took me to the Basilica of Guadalupe, sharing an experience of Our Lady from the heart of their own culture. I was moved, stunned, undone, and rewoven.

"You should talk about Her in your presentation tomorrow," one suggested, and the other vigorously agreed.

"I would not dare to speak of Her here in Mexico," I said. "I would feel not only like an outsider, but an imposter."

The two women looked at each other, clearly bewildered. "Don't you see?" one of them said. "Having someone from the outside share about what Our Lady means to her makes us all feel proud. Your love for Her is a gift to us." The other smiled, her eyes moist with tears.

In that moment I felt Guadalupe's tender kiss on the top of my head. Mindless cultural appropriation is a chronic malady. Love is always the remedy.

Washing the Wound

In 2022, I was scheduled to meet my friend Annie in Maui to share the stage at a conference honoring the legacy of Ram Dass. The venue required that everyone take a COVID test before flying to the island. Annie's came up positive. We were both heartbroken. Not only had we been preparing our collaboration with care, but we were looking forward to spending that week together in paradise. As the virus took her hostage, Annie surrendered to reality, and we stayed connected through the magic filament of our cell phones.

Curled up on her couch with a dog at her feet and a cup of tea beside her, Annie offered a steady stream of wise and funny insights distilled into texts that I shared onstage. I was carrying Annie in my pocket and sprinkling her over the gathering. The participants, who had been crushed with disappointment that Annie couldn't make it, sprang back to life. It felt like we were still teaching together. Our topic was "spiritual friendship." The idea was to lift our own relationship as an example of two people sharing the path of awakening, committed to mutual truth-telling, vulnerability, and accountability.

Meanwhile, I had let my friend down and didn't even realize it.

Just before I flew to Hawaii for a two-day board retreat leading up to the conference, Annie had sent me a draft of an essay from a new book she was writing. I was excited to read it, honored that she would offer me a sneak peek of a work in progress. I told her I'd read it on the plane. But, overwhelmed by the thousand details of getting out of town, I only skimmed it quickly, moved by its beauty and brilliance, and then set it aside, planning to give it my full attention once I got settled. But I neither settled nor returned to the manuscript. Instead, I was swept into the tumult of the event, where I was functioning as both a board member and a presenter, a magnet for an ongoing barrage of demands. And then I kind of . . . forgot.

After the workshop was over, Jeff and I rented a place on the beach for a week so that I could work on my own book and he could spend time in the arms of his mistress, the ocean. Every morning, after a long walk together, Jeff would stay on the beach to swim and watch waves, and I would return to the condo to write. I made good progress and felt gratified. On our last day, before flying home on the red-eye, we drove to a remote beach to go swimming. As I was drying off in the sun, a text came in from Annie.

"Did you ever get around to reading the piece I sent you?"

Oh my god. *No*. No, I did not. At least, not fully, and not with the care it deserved. Suddenly it felt like the sand was giving way under my legs, and I panicked. How could I have neglected to acknowledge such a gift? In my mind, Annie was being magnanimous by sharing a glimpse of her new project, and I was horrifically ungracious not to have responded. So, I pulled it up on my phone, and there on the hot sandy beach I read it from beginning to end. Sure enough, it was magnificent. In her signature style,

Annie had managed to convey an essential dharma teaching about the true nature of compassion dressed in the garb of an engaging story of an encounter with an unhoused person on a park bench that was both vulnerable and hilarious, precisely particular and utterly universal. With tears in my eyes, I texted her something kind but bland.

No answer.

So, a couple of days later I tried something more specific.

No response.

I let another week go by and then reached out again, asking her if I had caused her any pain by (1) waiting so long to read and respond to what she had shared, and then (2) being so brief in my response. I apologized and promised to be a better friend going forward. She wrote back to let me know that it hadn't hurt her feelings, but it had left her extremely anxious for a few days.

"I'm sure you know what my mind made of that silence," she said.

I sure did. One of the most naked feelings I know is when I choose someone with whom to share a draft of something I'm working on, especially when I suspect that I've struck gold and am equally terrified that it might be true and might not be.

Annie assured me that she had received the feedback she needed from other sources, and that everything between us was fine. Which did not stop me from plummeting into a shame vortex and letting it have its way with me all day long. Fortunately, decades of contemplative practice have given me just enough of a toehold on the cliff of self-hatred that I can observe my turmoil and not squander all my emotional cash to buy it. This allowed me to dig down under the fiery feelings to find the layers of shadow they were covering: *I don't matter. My opinions do not count. I am insignificant at best, and probably annoying. Annie sent me that piece to be nice. A widely acclaimed author gives a shit about what Mirabai Starr thinks? Highly unlikely. She is just throwing me a bone.* It wasn't a legitimate request from one writer to another; it was charity. And so, I had unconsciously let it slide.

Meanwhile, on Annie's end, my silence was a source of bewilderment and angst. She had carefully selected four people whose perceptions she trusts—among them her husband, her best friend (also an author), and a guy who has been her faithful beta reader for many years—and I was the only one who did not respond with substance, enthusiasm, and alacrity. She had "sent up a balloon" as she described it later, and when it thumped back to the ground, she understandably concluded that she wouldn't make that mistake again.

"After I got over the idea that you hated it, I figured you were just pathologically busy," Annie told me, "and that I was fourth or fifth on your list." Either way, not a recipe for trust with something as precious as an incipient book.

Which brought me to the next layer of shadow. For years now—decades—I have been setting and resetting my intention to simplify my life, and yet I remain frenetically overextended. Multiple losses haven't managed to make me change my ways. A cancer diagnosis didn't do it. Neither psychotherapy nor spiritual direction has succeeded in breaking this pattern. I am addicted to being busy. Busy makes me feel worthy. Like I'm paying some kind of rent for the space I take up in this world. I have blown up friendships because of this compulsion. Here was one such friendship, going up in flames before my eyes, and I felt powerless to save it.

"I want to explain to Annie that my negligence was about not believing my feedback matters and had nothing to do with the beauty and power of what she wrote," I told my friend SeiFu, "but that would be making this about me, and what I want more than anything is to make it about her." I declared that now that I had let some time elapse, I would write her an email, explaining my realization about why I had let her essay slip through the cracks. I was always at my best when I could hide behind the written word.

"You should call her," SeiFu said. "Have a real conversation."

I considered this terrifying proposition. What was the worst that could happen? She would respond with cold disdain, thank me politely for calling, and never speak to me again. Or simply decline to take my call, as if I were a telemarketer. And she would be more than justified in doing so. I never deserved a friend like Annie to begin with. Which she clearly had concluded herself. My monkey mind was off and running.

I texted her. "Good morning!" I chirped. "I'm wondering if we can talk on the phone sometime this week."

Within seconds she texted back. "Sure. I can talk right now if you're free."

Right now? I hadn't lined up my emotional ducks, picked out my words, shined up my armor.

I dialed her number.

I don't know if I've ever encountered anyone as willing to dive into the muck of human relationships as Annie. Her attention was as tangible as water pouring from the dipper of her deep listening into the cup I had drained with my self-loathing. She considered each disclosure, reflected it back to me. She identified with the "disease of perfectionism" that plagues me, how making a mistake (failing a friend, for example) feels like life and death. She recalled how not long ago she too was tyrannized by busyness, how life used to snap its fingers and she'd come running. Annie did not judge me for my participation in the human condition. She thanked me for being willing to open the box of shame and entrust her with its contents.

"Isn't it amazing to ease out of the pond together?" Annie marveled.

She shared some kind of medieval medical analogy having to do with wounds that seem to heal over while really the infection continues to fester under the surface, the pus growing hot and stinky. It needs to be lanced. Together we were making a deft slice in the flesh of our friendship and letting it drain. I thought this was an unnecessarily nasty way to describe the beautiful alchemy of our mutual truth-telling, but I often wish reality were prettier than it is.

"I'd pay anything for lancing this wound and splashing it with the antiseptic waters of our love for each other," Annie said, "and taking it back out into the sun."

It's understandable if you might want to do anything other than this uncomfortable business of trying to be truthful—reorganize the shed or take up knitting, for instance—but it's vital work. Mystical work. Annie calls it "cleansing the soul's windshield."

Once we remove those splattered bugs and wipe away the dust of the road, it's a lot safer to drive.

Not every friend is willing to do messy, smelly soul surgery with you. We can't expect that level of courage and curiosity. But if we can travel the wilderness of true soul companionship as intrepid explorers, climbing the closest hill to gain a vantage point when our comrades are too weary to move another inch, binding each other's blistered feet and taking turns building the fire at night, we participate in building beloved community, one relationship at a time.

Face to the Ground

It was a scorching day here in the high desert, where the sun seems much closer and blazes more brightly than it does at sea level. We gathered at the corner of the Taos Plaza and lay down in the busiest intersection of our small town. As a woman with a megaphone counted the minutes from one to nine-and-a-half, vehicles halted, engines idling, diesel smoke pluming. Sweat prickled my scalp and began to trickle down my jawline and pool at my lips.

Who knew that lying still could be so hard? I hadn't bothered to properly set this up. My face was smashed into the gravel, and I turned a little sideways so I could breathe better, vividly aware that George Floyd had not had the luxury of adjusting his head to suck extra air. Some pedestrians stopped to call out encouraging words. "Good job!" Or "Thank you for your activism!" Someone placed small plastic bottles of water among the crowd so that when we were finished with our protest we could hydrate. A guy in a pickup truck shouted, "Blacks are not the only ones oppressed! What about us Chicanos?" He ground his gears and roared away in the other direction.

Three minutes. Five. I started to cry.

I wept for everyone who belonged to any oppressed minority. Black people. Trans people. Black trans people. I wept for the persecution of my Jewish ancestors and for the Palestinians under occupation imposed by their descendants. For women burned as witches and for Native American children buried in unmarked graves behind government schools. And I cried because I felt so damned vulnerable lying there on my belly with my community prone all around me, or watching from the sidewalk, or wishing we'd get up off the ground so they could get on with their day.

When the nine-and-a-half minutes were over, we stood, brushed the dirt from our clothes and faces, and went home. All night I thrashed in my bed, helplessly reliving the horror of lying on hot pavement, thinking of George calling for his mama, wondering what good it could possibly do to stop traffic and pretend we couldn't breathe. The next morning, I woke up with a sore throat. By the end of that day, I had come down with a full-blown cold. I sat in the fire of my misery and realized that there is no answer to the problem of suffering. There is only the awkward, loving effort to practice solidarity with those who suffer. I carry both the ambiguity of privilege and the recognition of kinship. I saw that whether we engage in active protests or simply fling our small, heartbroken prayer for justice out into the hot summer sky, it will never be enough. But it is something. Our love matters.

We breathe together.

Practice
METTA (LOVINGKINDNESS MEDITATION)

Settle into a comfortable position, back straight but not rigid, eyes closed or gaze soft. Take a couple of full, conscious breaths, deepening the inhalation and lengthening the exhalation. Now, tenderly focusing on your own being, repeat to yourself: *May I be well. May I be happy. May I be safe. May I be at peace.* Feel free to amend the language to suit your aspirations. Extend lovingkindness to yourself as if you were your own best friend or lover, or a child.

Then shift your attention to someone you are deeply fond of, someone who has given you love. Picturing this person in your mind's eye, silently repeat your own version of these wishes: *May you be well. May you be happy. May you be safe. May you be at peace.* Connect with the warmth of heart this visualization evokes. Let it spread and glow through your whole body.

Next, picture someone you have trouble loving, a personal adversary or toxic public figure. Radiating warmth from the center of your chest, your spiritual heart, silently repeat your expressions of lovingkindness: *May you be well. May you be happy. May you be safe. May you be at peace.* Endeavor to mean it. Expand your capacity of heart beyond the opinions of your mind, and believe that your loving thoughts have the power to impact reality for the better.

At last, your heart softened and expansive from intentionally loving yourself and others, send lovingkindness out to the whole world: *May all beings be well. May all beings be happy. May all beings be safe. May all beings be at peace.*

Welcome whatever feelings arise during this practice—grief,

outrage, sweetness, or even apathy. There is no right or wrong way to offer yourself to the broken world, starting with the one who is often the most difficult to love: yourself.

⨯

WRITING PROMPT

Ode to an Unlikely Companion

Compose a poem in praise of someone (or something) you may find difficult to love.

SIX

Feeling

Broken Open

The Faces of Loss

Stop firing your feelings. They are the messengers of wisdom. Anger may contain information about boundaries you have allowed to be transgressed for too long, infusing you with the energy to start asking for what you need. Your despair can connect you to the suffering of the world, cracking open your heart so that compassion for all beings can flow in. Moments of contentment are wrapped gifts from the universe. Untie them. In Spanish, *Estoy emocionada* means "I'm excited." The thrill of emotion is entwined with something wonderful. Grief can be the most potent feeling of all, and the one from which society tries its best to distract us. And yet it is a crucible for transformation. Inside the well of sorrow our souls are remade.

There are many faces of loss. A beloved pet dies, a relationship breaks up, a friend betrays you, a community rejects you. A serious health diagnosis signals the end of a life you knew. There is loss of innocence, loss of financial security, loss of your active role as a parent when a child grows up and leaves home. Each loss is an invitation to inhabit the sacred space of the unknown. Mystics of all traditions tell us that the unknown is the place where we come to know God.

Grief is not a malady to be cured or an error to be corrected. It is a natural response to a life-altering loss. When we choose to stay present in the fire of suffering, rather than turn away, self-medicate, or try to "fix" it through "spiritual bypassing" (using beliefs and practices to check out of reality), it can become a threshold to sacred space. Our broken hearts break us open to deeper love. "Certainly nothing breaks us, aches us, and wakes us like grief," says my soul-sister Joanne Cacciatore,[1] professor of social work at Arizona State University, who has dedicated her life to walking us home through the landscape of loss. "Listen to the holiness that underpins grief, the sacred that, when held in unconditional compassion, opens us— and wakes us—to more."

Vulnerable

One of the longest walks I ever took was from the parking lot to the doorway of my first grief support group. I kept getting out of my car,

---

1 Cacciatore, Joanne. *Bearing the Unbearable: Love, Loss, and the Heartbreaking Path of Grief.* Wisdom Publications, 2017.

walking toward the entrance to the furniture store where the group was gathering, and rushing back to the car and flinging myself inside.

It was a new car. My daughter had crashed my old one when she died. I had not yet made it into a nest on wheels. But it was still more comfortable than a room full of bereaved strangers. It was safer than saying out loud, "My child is dead." To walk through that door was to acknowledge the reality of my loss. I wasn't ready.

But I was. I was ready. Ready to turn my face toward the blaze. I had nothing left to lose.

So, I finally walked all the way in and the kindly man leading the group, whom I happened to have met when we both taught middle school and neither of our daughters had died yet, leapt out of his chair and scooped me into a hug.

"We're glad you're here," he said.

Suddenly I was glad, too. I could immediately tell that I had entered a sanctuary where no one expected me to be okay, where everyone was as shattered as I was, and where I could talk about my loss without feeling like people were getting sick of hearing about it. I took refuge in our shared vulnerability.

Sometimes the boldest and most transformative thing we can do is allow ourselves to be vulnerable. To lay down the burden of the stiff upper lip and keen. And yet it is wise to be discerning about when and to whom you reveal the jewel of your broken heart. My friend Patty, a death educator and grief counselor, says, "People have to earn the privilege of our vulnerability." Sharing your pain with someone who does not reciprocate with reverence and tenderness can catapult you back into anguish, rather than create a space for you to come safely undone and replenish your depleted soul.

When I took my seat in that first grief circle, it was a home-coming. The first night, I did not even say anything. I just quietly cried, and more experienced mourners nodded and smiled with their eyes. By the second week, I started to feel like I had found my clan. There was a Chicana cocktail waitress wearing tight jeans with bling on the pockets and more makeup than I had ever seen on a single face. I was teaching philosophy at the university, and she had dropped out of school at age fifteen to have a baby—the same eighteen-year-old baby whose recent death by accidental drug overdose she was now here to grieve. There was a man from Taos Pueblo whose sister was dying of uterine cancer and who had his whole tribe to support him but said he came for the cookies. There was a heterosexual couple whose baby had died at birth, and another couple of women who had spent their family's retirement funds on in vitro fertilization, and nothing had worked so they were giving up. There was the vet tech with half a dozen dogs of her own, but when her Rottweiler died she felt she could not live without him.

Outside the walls of that little back room, with piles of oriental rugs in one corner and a cluster of mismatched lamps in another, we had nothing in common. But the moment the circle was opened and the talking stick was passed, I felt more seen and accepted, heard and protected, than I did among my closest friends, all of whom were trying hard but none of whom could quite understand.

Choose carefully the ones who are worthy of the gift of your vulnerability. But choose. Dare to be naked, offering the tender pink of your flayed heart to the human family. Remember that we belong to each other. And that your turn will come again to be a listening pool into which someone else can spill their holy tears.

He Has Given You His Love-Light to Carry

How

by Rosemerry Wahtola Trommer

How do we live at the traumatic center of death and life?
—Rabbi Irwin Kula, Original Thinkers Festival 2022

A single moment contains
the scent of warm pumpkin pie
and the gravedigger's spade,
the splatter of blood
and the smooth honeyed flesh of mango.
Did we ever believe we would live
this life unscathed?
Oh, the stab of loss
and the clean, mineral perfume of rain.
Oh, the ache of loss
and the deep golden sunflowered yes.
Oh, the carving of loss
and the sweet subtle tang of apples in fall.
Oh, the ache, oh, the ache,
oh, the beauty, the loss,
oh, the beauty, the loss, oh, the beauty.

A couple of decades ago, a young poet named Rosemerry committed to writing a poem a day. She began with an organic version of mindfulness practice. She would show up for exactly what is—a colicky baby who literally cried every waking moment, a layer of ice floating on the river outside her Colorado home, the fragrance rising from a cup of steaming Earl Grey tea—and then she would distill the essence of her observations into a poem. She banished perfectionism and relinquished control. She allowed herself to be surprised.

Eventually, Rosemerry's willingness to not know what was next opened into a love affair with the present moment. She shifted from trying to write something *good* to wanting to write something *true*. She began to publish her poems online in the form of a blog called *A Hundred Falling Veils* and quickly gathered a wide following of poetry lovers and seekers of the wisdom embodied right here in the ordinary extraordinary moments of our lives. Thinning carrots in the garden, paying bills online, watching children sleep. The tagline is "There's a poem in every day." By inviting us to bear witness to her discoveries, Rosemerry entices us to uncover the poem nestled in the heart of our own everyday existence. Poetry becomes a mystical experience, a way of meeting the world as it is and discovering the sacred flaming from the heart of the common. This is great when the stakes are relatively low, but what about when the most difficult of all experiences breaks down the doors of your life and, with the precision of a sword, strips and flays you?

A few weeks before his seventeenth birthday, Rosemerry's son Finn died by suicide. He did not exactly plan it, yet in many ways his spontaneous choice was not a surprise. Finn had struggled with his complicated mind and mighty heart all his life. Opposite impulses were woven into the swirl of his soul. He was serious and obsessive, playful and silly. He was a classical dancer who listened to cello music and aspired to join the military. He loved his life. And when he saw a gun among the boxes of a relative whom he was helping to move into a new apartment, he made a choice to end it.

His mother's poetry practice did not keep her grief from lighting her life on fire. But it did teach her how to burn. It teaches her still. She is discovering that she doesn't need to protect herself against the truth—the truth of her vulnerability, of her devastation, of her longing—and that she couldn't fend it off if she tried. As it turns out, she is grateful to meet what is real inside herself and in the world. "The moment I see something I don't want to be true," Rosemerry tells me, "I hear, 'Of course you don't, sweetheart,' and the tenderness of this inner voice gives me the strength to remember that I don't have to carry all this on my own." She describes a feeling I too had when my child died, that she is being carried by Love itself—which usually takes the form of other people, nature, language, and silence. "All I had to do was nothing," Rosemerry says. "Zero effort." This surrender is countercultural. And it is at the heart of the path of the ordinary mystic.

There is a magical suburban street that winds through Rosemerry's story. Only two nights before Finn died, mother and son were out walking, leaning close together and laughing, listening to the frogs with their baritone burbling in a nearby pond, smelling marijuana fumes wafting from an open window, exclaiming in wonderment at the fireflies sparkling in the warm night air. In that moment, Rosemerry realized that every second of her life was worth that hour of walking and laughing with her beautiful boy. (Of course, she promptly wrote a poem about it.)

The morning after Finn's death, Rosemerry was walking on that same street when what she describes as "a tidal wave of love" rose above her and she saw that it was about to annihilate her. "No!" her soul screamed. But the wave crashed over her anyway. "It had nothing to do with my no," she tells me. "It was Love. And like a comet dispersing into shooting stars, my grief shattered into small parts and each one was wrapped in love so that I could meet it, carry it, even welcome it."

That night, Rosemerry went out walking again, this time reeling in anguish, and she suddenly recalled the sweetness of their walk a few days earlier, the easy joy between them. She realized that nothing—not even the violence of Finn's suicide—could take away the perfection of that moment. It would live inside her always, a small beam of comfort penetrating the well of grief.

That's when her cell phone rang. It was a dear friend who had just heard the news. Rosemerry cannot recall much about their conversation, other than the wave of care that scooped her up and held her together, but she does remember her friend saying this: "He has given you his love-light to carry." In that instant, a firefly lit up in front of Rosemerry's face. She laughed out loud. *Yes! He is giving me his love-light to carry.*

Three months later, another visitation, a fresh affirmation, a continued invitation to inhabit the mystery. Rosemerry had returned to visit family for the first time since Finn died, and she had spent the afternoon sitting in the spot where he had taken his life, allowing herself to feel everything, pushing nothing away. After dinner, exhausted, stilled, replete, she took her now customary walk. It grew late, but she wasn't ready to go back into the house where she had last seen her son alive. She lay down in the grass and looked up. In that moment, an enormous shooting star arced across the sky and she heard Finn's voice: "I'm not in there, Mom. I'm out here." That was it exactly. Finn was a comet. He had flashed across the horizon of her life with brilliance and violence, power and beauty, and then he was gone.

Eventually, these external messages shifted inward and became more integrated with her life. One day, longing for contact with her son, Rosemerry called out to him, "Are you here?" She sent her feelers out into the atmosphere, hoping to detect his presence. That's when she felt a kind of knocking from the inside, as if Finn were tapping inside her chest. She understood this to mean, *Not out there, Mom. In here. Always in here.* Since then, Rosemerry has felt that Finn is always with her, whether there are signs or not.

For the ordinary mystic, even the most shattering losses can be portals to the sacred. Grief tears open the fabric of our hearts, and into that vastness the mystery of love comes seeping, permeating the ravaged landscape of our lives and blessing it. Grief unravels and rethreads us. That doesn't make our heartbreaks good news. But the way of the mystic invites you to slow down and allow for the possibility that from the depths of a pain greater than you can bear a greater love than you could have dreamed of is calling your name.

Ancestors

A miraculous thing sometimes happens after our loved ones have left this world: they turn into saints, and we spontaneously begin to worship them. Maybe not saints in any conventional sense, but they become luminous. Unconditionally loving. They pervade the fibers of our hearts and deepen the way we perceive the world. The veils of personality have dropped, and true essence has been revealed. Some might call this magical thinking; I say it's the opposite. When we see the beauty and goodness of our loved ones who have died, we are seeing reality. It's harder to glimpse the real behind the trappings of character quirks when the person is alive. They could be boring or mean, no doubt about it. Maybe your partner smoked too much pot and checked out of the relationship, or your teenager was sarcastic. Your mom was hypercritical and your dad didn't have a paternal bone in his body. But it seems our loved ones behave much better on the Other Side. Now that they are no longer confined to bodies and egos, their presence expands like the warmth of the sun as it lifts above the horizon in the morning. We feel them everywhere, and they bless us.

The late Zen bard Leonard Cohen challenged the psychological trope that when we fall in love, we are projecting our own fantasies onto the blank screen of another person, and that when we fall out of love, we are seeing the other for who they really are. Instead, according to Saint Leonard, it is the true essence of the person— luminous and delightful—that we fall in love with. But it is difficult to sustain that heightened state of seeing, and so we let the veils drop and obscure our loved one's essential beauty and goodness. Similarly, when people we deeply care about are no longer alive, they reveal their magnificence. Why wouldn't we fall on our knees and praise them?

When my daughter died, I had the sensation that she had become my ancestor. Our roles reversed and now she was watching over me, looking after my well-being, guiding my steps. She occupies the same space in my psyche as my grandmother, a benevolent presence I can call upon when I am grappling with a quandary or about to initiate a project. I am not the only bereaved parent I have heard express this bewildering phenomenon of spiritual role reversal. Whether this is one way our shattered hearts try to make sense of the senseless or an actual manifestation of a new reality doesn't matter to me. My child is one of my spirit guides now, and I am grateful.

Spirit Plate

It was Jenny's birthday. She would have been turning eighteen. I had been speaking at a grief conference in Arizona, which was both the most comforting and the most real place I could be on this difficult day when my baby wouldn't be aging but would remain forever fourteen. My friend Ted, who lost not one but two children in a car wreck a few years before I lost Jenny, took me out to dinner. We sat outside, under the cool spray of the misters, marveling at the difference in temperature between Scottsdale and our mountain town of Taos.

When we ordered, Ted asked for an extra plate, and when the food came, he created a spirit plate, arranging bits of salad, pasta, and garlic bread for the invisible birthday girl. We sprinkled a couple of drops of wine from my glass and Seven Up from his on top. He asked for a piece of cake with a candle, and we sang "Happy Birthday." When we were finished eating, Ted slipped out the patio gate and knelt to lay the offering under a flowering crab apple tree before bringing it back to the table to be cleared by the busboy. It was the first time in four years that I didn't feel like Jenny's birthday might kill me.

This is what ritual is for. Ritual honors the dead and helps the living live. Traditional cultures are way better at this than modern American society. But we can respectfully draw from the generous wellspring of the world's wisdom to help us navigate the sacred landscape of loss if our own culture lacks meaningful death rituals. Many such ceremonies involve food. In the Hindu tradition, you always first offer to the guru and the gods the food you prepare, and then serve it to the humans. That's not because the disembodied beings deserve to eat first. It's because when you raise a plate of food in homage and thanksgiving, the deities bless it and it comes back to you as soul sustenance. For a devout Catholic, receiving communion is literally partaking of the body and blood of Christ.

In Judaism, we sit shiva for seven days following the funeral of a close beloved. Friends and relatives come to the house bearing trays of food and bottles of drink. They do not try to cheer us up or distract us from the holy task of mourning. They sit beside us. They pray with us or abide in silence with us, or they listen while we talk about our loved one, stories from their life or accounts of their dying, and sprinkle in an anecdote or two of their own. They arrange food on a plate, pour a cup of tea and set it before us. "Eat a little," they urge. Maybe we do. Maybe we can't. But we are not expected to think about feeding ourselves. All our energy and attention are focused on being present for the momentous event of our loved one's death.

Death is not always deemed a disaster. Dia de los Muertos (Day of the Dead) is one of the most festive occasions in Latin American communities, weaving pre-Columbian Indigenous practices with Christian beliefs. Over the course of two days, November first and second, families and friends gather to remember loved ones who have died. They create *ofrendas*, household altars with pictures of the deceased; brightly painted sugar skulls; objects that were important to them, such as books and rosaries, garlands of fresh marigolds; and the foods and drinks they loved best: tortilla chips and tomatillo salsa, maybe, tres leches cake or Snickers bars, tequila and apple soda. They head en masse to the village *camposanto* (cemetery) and perch on the tombstones, drinking beer, laughing, and blasting music from portable speakers. They may tell embarrassing stories about the person who died, teasing them as if sharing the joke in real time.

Our Zapotec friends in Oaxaca ring bells throughout the village to call the spirits of the dead. They lay paths of marigolds from their courtyards to the street so that their loved ones can find their way home. They place cups of water so the dead can refresh themselves and pairs of glasses so they can see the living. They invite the spirits to a feast in their honor. And when the last dishes are collected and washed, the bottles are empty and the instruments are put away, they ring the bells again, so the spirits of the dead, now fully fed and tenderly loved, can slip back to the Other Side.

As an everyday mystic, you are welcome to create rituals for everything that matters. Make up a ceremony when your first grandchild is born and invite all your friends to offer their blessings. Create a spirit shrine at your wedding, placing photographs of your father or your partner's baby sister, so that loved ones who have died can be included in your special day. If you run a marathon, dedicate it to someone you love who is no longer alive. Paint and write and sing for the dead. When you gather for family holidays, light a candle for someone you all wish could be with you. Don't pretend the empty chair isn't there.

Lady on the Wall

When he was ten and I was seven, my big brother, Matty, died of a brain tumor.

It was December of 1968, and by then Mom had given birth to two more children, my sister, Amy, and my brother Roy. Matty woke up in the middle of the night with a headache, and nine months later he was gone. Amy had just turned four and Roy was an infant.

Matty's death planted a seed for one of the ways I have come to God ever since—through the doorway of death. The other one is beauty: art, music, poetry, wild nature. Beauty and death have been my portals to the sacred.

I wouldn't have named this experience God, though. God was not a popular word in my agnostic household. Plus, I was young enough that there was nothing that wasn't God. The world was still magical, the veil between this reality and the invisible one translucent. What I knew is that Matty had been gathered up into a space that was mysterious and important, and that all I could do was stand before the threshold in awe and behave myself. I also knew that in some way Matty was with me still, and that if I talked about him, it would keep him close.

So, I did. I talked about him incessantly. With my third-grade teacher when I went back to school after Christmas break. With the girls in my class who had heard the news, and any boys who slowed down enough for me to catch them and tell them about my dead brother. With the dentist and the postman and our cousins visiting from California. Someone gave us a portable tape recorder and I leaned in, telling every Matty story I could remember and making up the rest (man, do I wish I knew what became of that recording of my eight-year-old grieving self). I asked my mother about every detail of his final days, even though she cried as she described the way he fought for his life and lost. Her tears felt holy to me. I asked my father if Matty was afraid to die and he said he didn't think so and I believed him. I reminded my sister about how Matty would do his best Woody Woodpecker impersonations just for her, hoping she would never forget how her big brother made her laugh. And I made sure my baby brother knew that Matty, knowing he might die soon, had named him after his favorite baseball player, Roy White (a Black man), sealing their bond forever.

In those early days after his funeral, I couldn't fall asleep. I would turn myself over and over, my pillow too hot, my pajamas jumbled. One night, I slipped out of my bed in the room I shared with Amy and made my way down the hall to Matty's room. I climbed onto his empty bed, rolled onto my side, and stared at the wall, willing him to make an appearance and talk to me. But it was not Matty I saw. Instead, the face of a woman came into focus, dark skin framed by long dark curls blending into the dark wall, dark eyes peering into mine. I did not move. She didn't speak, but she communicated.

The Lady was neither gentle nor harsh. She was strong, and she wanted me to know that she had always been with me and always would be, and that she had been with Matty, too. If I was afraid, I could ask her to protect me, and if I missed my brother, she would tell him for me. This wasn't entirely good news. The Lady intimidated me, and I didn't have any reason to trust her. But, propelled by curiosity and longing, I came back the next night and there she was, and she showed up on all the other nights I crept into Matty's bed to reach him through her. After a while, Matty's room was repurposed as the nursery for baby Roy, and the Lady faded. I began to wonder whether she had ever really been there at all.

Maybe it doesn't matter whether there are actual invisible advocates who carry us when we cannot walk ourselves through the wilderness of grief. The important thing is to let yourself be reached.

Hold Me

When the scaffolding of your life collapses, as it inevitably will, mystical wisdom invites you to sit very still inside the wreckage. Nothing else makes sense anymore. Online sales events or the fluctuating numbers on the bathroom scale, what to make for dinner or whether to repaint the kids' room. You probably know enough by now, because life has been a fierce and skillful teacher, to not try running away from reality. You deepen your breath and look around. Gingerly, and with self-compassion.

Maybe someone you loved very much has died. Or someone from whom you were estranged. Either way, death feels so final, what is done cannot be undone, and something of who you used to be died with that person. It could be that a serious injury has re-configured all your plans. Or a career you have cultivated jumps its tracks and loses all meaning and now you don't know who you are anymore. Perhaps your partner lit your relationship on fire, incin-erating all your romantic dreams. Yes, you have the courage to face the pain. You have tools—psychological techniques and spiritual methodologies—but they have their limits.

When you cannot hold yourself, ask your community to hold you. Beseech them. Do not take no for an answer. Chances are, if you call out, they will come running. It's not easy. You probably don't want to be a bother, broken little you, with your obsessions and your trembling. Or you are so shattered, you simply don't have the energy to ask. Try. Fling your whispered plea into the field. Someone will pick it up, call on the others, and they will gather. Especially in times of catastrophe. We are good at that, humans. We rebuild each other's burnt barns.

My friend Wendy is a writing teacher whose son took his own life a few years after her husband took his. When she could not muster up any meaning from this pileup of violent losses, her com-munity made meaning for her. How? By explaining that everything is perfect if only she had eyes to see? By instructing her in medita-tion practices and encouraging her to go to church? Nope. They held her by picking up her dirty laundry and returning it clean and folded. By pouring her a glass of apple juice and sitting beside her as she drank it. By crying with her. And mostly this way: Wendy was too broken to pray, so she asked her people to pray for her. And they did. And it helped.

It's not perfect, but it's real. Even if you can't feel it (because you can't feel anything), it's happening. Your losses touch multiple circles of people, and with the inrush of their breath, you are lifted a little. I remember complaining to my friend Elaine that a few weeks after my daughter Jenny died everyone got back to their regular lives and left me behind in a bleeding bundle. In her characteristically blunt manner, Elaine set me straight.

"Stop it, Mirabai. Don't you realize that tons of people are praying for you right now? You are being held by a circle of friends you are too sad to see. But they're there. We're here."

A few years later, Elaine's seemingly healthy forty-year-old son died of a heart attack while playing soccer in the park with his daughter and her friends. Elaine got to have her turn collapsing into the invisible arms of community. And we held her as best we could.

Look. You don't have to do anything when your world comes undone. Who could expect you to mend your own broken bones? Call on us, the ones who love you, the close friends and distant acquaintances, old adversaries and new co-workers. Say, "I cannot pray right now. Will you please pray for me?" Or, "I have zero faith in a God who could allow this to happen. But you seem to. Please, do your thing." And then lie down on the ground. The earth herself will hold you.

Prison and Plague

Like every other mystic on the planet, including you, Saint Francis of Assisi had to endure tribulation to be transformed. See if you can relate. In his youth, Francis was a party animal, drinking with his buddies, hitting on women, playing loud music, spending his parents' money. Francis was conscripted to fight in a battle between his hometown of Assisi and the neighboring community of Perugia (which would not be unlike Brooklyn going to war against the Bronx, but this was not uncommon in the Middle Ages). He was taken captive as a prisoner of war, thrown into a cell, and held for ransom.

It was during his captivity that Francis began to engage God in conversation. I like to imagine that at first he was just messing around, passing the time, pretending there was someone there on the other end listening to Francis and nodding their holy head. But little by little, Francis grew quiet enough to hear the true voice of the divine. The relationship became real, the intimacy deepened, and the love began to pervade every fiber of Francis's being. When he was released from prison, his addictions fell away, and he dedicated himself to the alleviation of suffering among the poorest of the poor.

The sixteenth-century Spanish mystic John of the Cross was also broken open by incarceration. Persecuted for supporting his mentor, Teresa of Avila, in reforming the corrupted Carmelite Order, he was yanked out of his bed in the middle of the night, taken to a remote monastery, and crammed into a tiny, windowless cell where he languished for nine months. John saved his sanity by composing poetry in his head and committing it to memory. His poems were drenched in love-longing. He cried out to a God he no longer even believed in, and the tension between faith and doubt shattered his soul and allowed the light to come flooding in.

I can relate. When I was a young girl, poetry saved me too. Writing it, singing it, reading it. My darkest times revealed the most luminous jewels when I leaned in and paid attention.

The medieval English mystic Lady Julian of Norwich, the first woman to be published in the English language, lived through the most savage years of the plague. By most estimates, the Black Death eradicated half the inhabitants of Europe. It swept through the population in waves. People would just be starting to regain their equilibrium and it would strike again. Although there is no biographical information about Julian, we can surmise (and I do) that she was a grieving widow and a bereaved mother. Julian knew sorrow in the depths of her bones. She wanted to die, she admits at the beginning of her *Revelations of Divine Love*.

But Julian didn't die. Instead, she had a near-death experience in which Christ revealed himself as an unconditionally loving mother, assuring her so that she could reassure the world that, against all evidence to the contrary, "all will be well and all will be well and every kind of thing shall be well." Can you take this in, take it all the way into your own aching heart? For Julian, it was not a matter of exercising the power of positive thinking. Like all mystics, she had direct experience of the sacred bubbling up from beneath the ravaged landscape of her soul, and it filled her heart with "merriment." Julian chose to spend the rest of her life as an anchoress, "sheltering in place" and unpacking her sixteen "showings" for the benefit of sorrowing souls for generations to come.

Imprisonment. Plague. These were the terrible gardens in which some of the world's greatest mystical geniuses grew. What are your own fierce portals? The suicide of a loved one; your own suicidal thoughts? Chronic pain, mental illness, addiction? Are you in an abusive relationship and cannot find a way to extricate yourself, though you have tried? You are not alone. Luminaries have walked before you, and they can light your way. But before you walk, you must stop, drop to your knees, and listen. Under the cracked desert floor, an aquifer is surging.

Saint Gladys

Known as the Little Flower, the nineteenth-century saint Thérèse of Lisieux embodied a spirituality of naked simplicity and childlike wonderment that serves as an antidote to the complex theological doctrines and abstract philosophical notions that leave most of us out in the cold. Thérèse aspired to disappear in the holy riot of creation. "If every flower wanted to be a rose," she said, "nature would lose its springtime beauty." When I was in my early twenties, living on the outskirts of a remote village in Mexico's Yucatan Peninsula, I met a woman named Gladys who embodied Thérèse's example of the Little Way, investing the most ordinary tasks of everyday life as love-offerings to God.

Gladys was around ten years older than I was. She was small and thin, with dark brown skin and an incandescent smile. She came to help me out in the eco-lodge my parents had built on the shore of Laguna Bacalar near the border of Belize. My job was a disorganized combination of cooking, cleaning, and tending to the needs of the few guests who found their way to our jungle enclave. The first time we met, Gladys reached up and buttoned my sweater. "You must not get sick," she said, and then patted my face. It was a cool night for the tropics, but that meant the temperature had plummeted from maybe eighty degrees to seventy-two.

From that moment on, Gladys made it her mission to take care of me, making me sit down and eat when she felt I was working too hard, sewing torn seams in my flowing sundress ("So much fabric!" she exclaimed in awe, fingering the wasted material), greeting me with a lingering embrace every morning when she showed up for work, and hugging me again when she left at the end of the day. Gladys behaved as if it were an incredible stroke of luck to be able to scramble other people's eggs and squeeze their orange juice, to empty the bathroom trash and fetch my sunglasses from across the compound. I was wary at first of her childlike devotion, but I soon realized she was authentic and came to rely on my daily dose of Gladys-love.

A few weeks after Gladys was hired, she showed up with a middle-aged man and introduced him as her friend Manuel. "You need a night watchman here," she said. "Manuel is the perfect person to look out for your property."

I conferred with my parents and they agreed. Our tiny eco-retreat was slowly growing, and we finally had something to protect. Besides, it was the custom in Mexico to have a guard at hotels, and we were trying to be respectful of the culture. We hired Manuel. He proved to be an ideal night watchman. He was vigilant and kindly. Where Gladys bubbled over with sweet chatter, Manuel was largely silent. They balanced each other, and for a time our little staff exuded harmony.

One morning, Gladys did not show up for work. I made do without her and assumed she'd be back the next day. But she wasn't.

So I climbed into the enormous ranch pickup and drove the five kilometers to her house and knocked on the door. After a long pause, Gladys opened the door. I asked how she was feeling and inquired whether or not she thought she would be available for the large party (twelve whole guests) that was scheduled to arrive that evening for a bird-watching tour. She shook her head, looking down.

"I do not know when I will be returning," Gladys whispered. She kept dabbing at the corners of her mouth with a twisted bandana. She didn't touch me. She was folded in on herself.

I knew this was too good to be true, I admonished myself. Everyone warned me—even the locals—that people here take advantage of well-meaning gringos who are too stupid to erect proper boundaries with the people who work for them. I had often been accused of letting my earnest liberal sensibilities snooker me. I should have known better. I was making Gladys into a saint, I thought, but she was just a regular human who takes what she wants and then moves on.

I assumed the most lordly stance and formal tone I could muster and let Gladys know that in the future it was imperative that she provide me with advance warning if she didn't think she would be making it in to work. She nodded again, eyes still downcast. I did not hug her. I said nothing reassuring. I got back in my silly truck and drove away.

That afternoon, Elvia, who lived with her family in the caretaker's house on my mom's property in the village, sauntered up to me as I was preparing to make dinner for the bird-watchers.

"¿Escuchaste el chisme calienete?" she asked, wondering if I had heard the "hot gossip." Her eyes were alight with drama.

"*¿Cuál chisme?*" I asked, too busy to be that interested.

"Gladys," she said. "She killed herself."

My heart thundered and my head whirled. "What? Are you sure? Why?"

"That man she was in love with. Her parents did not approve, because he was a *campesino*." Elvia faked a sad smile. "They thought he was taking advantage of Gladys because of . . . how she was."

"How she was?"

"You know, *simple*." Elvia tapped on her head.

So that sweetness and caring I associated with enlightenment was seen by her community as a mental disability.

Without a word to Elvia, ignoring my obligations in the kitchen, I jumped back in the pickup and raced along the jungle highway to the house where Gladys, as it turned out, had been living with her parents and her two small children ever since her husband had left them two years earlier. My Gladys, I was to discover, had secrets. Manuel and Gladys, for example, had been carrying on an affair. She arranged to get him the job as our night watchman so that she could sneak back over to the lodge when everyone was asleep and spend the night with him. Manuel, tired of living a lie, had ended the relationship the day before. Gladys had already ingested a bottle of rat poison when she met me at the door. She was gone an hour later.

When I arrived at Gladys's parents' home the evening of her suicide, the doorway was draped in black crepe, tied with a large black bow. Gladys's body was laid out on the dining room table in an open casket, her hands folded at her breast, her countenance soft. The room was dimly lit with large taper candles. Family and friends, dressed in black, spoke in muted voices. A circle of elderly women sat around Gladys's body, praying the rosary: *Dios te salve, María. Llena eres de gracia . . . Bendita tú eres entre todas las mujeres . . . Santa María, Madre de Dios, ruega por nosotros pecadores, ahora y en la hora de nuestra muerte. Amen.*

No one greeted me when I stepped across the threshold nor said goodbye when I slipped away.

Gladys was buried outside the sanctified ground of the church in a graveyard reserved for sinners, but she was the most beatific person I had ever met. Nearly forty years later, I still call on Gladys's kindness when it would be easier to close down my heart. When I want to judge people, I try to give them the benefit of the doubt; they may be suffering in ways I will never know. When I'm tempted to be cynical, I give myself over to my inner child, as Gladys did. I endeavor to treat strangers like family and button up their sweaters even when it isn't that cold out.

I am not championing suicide. But I'm not condemning it, either. I do not believe that the choice to end one's life is a violation of a sacred contract with the One who created it. What I do believe is that if we stay present when things feel most hopeless, allowing ourselves to become as curious as we are miserable, we will discover new freedom on the other side of any unbearable moment. Easier said than done, I realize. Biochemistry is powerful. Our brains can lay siege, and it can be nearly impossible to not believe what we are thinking. If you are contemplating suicide, I ask you to remember the words of Julian of Norwich, who, having lived through the Black Death and lost almost everyone she loved, still had the holy chutzpah to declare, "All will be well and all will be well and every kind of thing shall be well." Whisper these words to your own sweet self. And imagine your hand nestled in mine.

Loss and Longing

Once we have exhausted ourselves in the fruitless effort to keep grief at bay, we collapse into the arms of the darkness and let it have its way with us. We have nothing left to lose. We yield to reality, taking a long, sober look at what is and conceding what isn't. We have lost what we've lost, and there's no going back to the way things were before the Great Shattering. There is nowhere to turn except toward the unknown. We begin to befriend the mystery.

The whiff of this liminal space, this threshold zone, this ambiguous state of being, is subtly intoxicating. Even if it is pervaded by sadness, tinged with rage, laced with fear, it carries something that reminds our souls of their separation from their divine source, and it sparks within us a desire to return. As we allow that ember to intensify, it catches flame and we find ourselves filled with an ineffable yearning. Missing a loved one who has died or a partner who has left begins to resemble longing for the divine. Even if we do not subscribe to a belief system that postulates the existence of a personified being called God, there is no denying the connection between loss and longing, between grief and sacred desire. We may no longer know what we even want, but we begin wanting it with every fiber of our broken open heart.

This is what it is to walk as a mystic in this world. It's about continuously tuning the instrument of your soul so that it can pick up divine impulses and transmit them. It's about "keeping your heart open in hell," as my friend Stephen Levine used to say. It's about allowing our sorrow to ruin the walls that separate us from the rest of creation. We climb over the rubble and step into the landscape of belonging.

Practice
TONGLEN

"Taking and Sending" Visualization
(with thanks to Pema Chödrön)

———

Sit comfortably, with your spine aligned and your gaze turned inward. Take three full breaths. Inhale as deeply as you can, hold the inhalation for as long as you can, and then breathe out as slowly as you can. Feel the way your conscious breathing washes through every cell. Connect with that feeling of the breath in your body. Become intimate with it.

Now picture someone, somewhere, who is suffering. It may be a person you know, one you've only heard about, or even someone you read about or saw in the news. It may be a physical issue or an emotional one. Maybe both. Allow this person's pain to touch your heart. Let it in. Believe in your own capacity to contain the suffering of another. Feeling their pain will not kill you. It will not damage you. Your heart will expand to hold their burden with ease.

Begin to breathe in their pain. Visualize their suffering as dark, hot, and heavy. On the outbreath, extend relief. Visualize a bright, refreshing buoyancy filling the space left behind. You breathe in their specific distress and breathe out peace and compassion.

Imagine that your breath is medicine, is sunlight, is direct loving touch, with the power to alleviate suffering. Trust that the basic goodness of your own heart is powerful enough to transmute their pain, leaving no vestiges. The only impact of this practice is increasing your compassion. Include yourself in this circle of care. Know that whatever you are going through, countless others are experiencing a similar version of your unique suffering at this very moment. Allow your distress to connect you with the tender embrace of the human family.

✳

WRITING PROMPT

If only . . .

SEVEN

Unfolding

The Restless Butterfly

Looking Through the Eyes of Love

To be an ordinary mystic is to be on the lookout for magic, for moments of synchronicity and heartbreak, moments when common experiences like thundershowers and broken bones unexpectedly connect you to the whole cosmos and you fleetingly perceive the perfection of all that is. We've all had those glimpses. We may not have named them "mystical," but they are! If being a mystic is about becoming one with the One, then anything—*anything*—that leads to a unitive experience counts as mystical. It may happen in a Zendo or a cathedral, but it's just as likely (and just as valid) to happen in the marriage bed and on the deathbed. Once you have known that you are not separate from the universe, it is difficult to Otherize, to winnow the worthy from the unworthy, to see yourself as victim or conqueror.

Moments of "oneing" are not always dramatic. Maybe you take a dose of your favorite hallucinogen and experience yourself exploding through the veil of duality and dissolving into the ocean of unity, forever changing the way you perceive the cosmos and your place in it. But mystical moments can also be subtle, and often are. They sneak up on you. There you are, harvesting cherry tomatoes from your rooftop garden. The sun is coming up and the buildings on the other side of the street are washed in rosy light. It reminds you of the time you took a road trip to New Mexico with your ex-boyfriend and someone told you that the red color that spreads over the eastern mountains at sunset gave rise to the name Sangre de Cristo. The Blood of Christ Mountains! Which makes you remember how deeply in love you were at the time, how every touch felt like magic, and your heart fills with an ache of longing, but it isn't for him (he turned out to be a jerk) but for God. And in that same breath of yearning, you are filled with a sense of the divine presence, and you simply, quietly know that you are not exiled from this essence. It's delicate, this realization, like air, so you barely notice it. Yet it is as real as the hair on your head. This is a mystical experience. They are as common as dandelions, and as wondrous.

The more you make yourself available for mystical moments, the more they come flowing into the open field of your everyday life. As you cultivate a contemplative gaze, through meditation or prayer, with gratitude and forgiveness, you begin to taste the sacred in the most mundane: folding laundry, walking out the front door and heading to the car, choosing a loaf of bread at the market. It takes practice to look through the eyes of love.

At first, you may feel like a newly hatched butterfly who stumbles around, shaking your wings, unsure of their function, lifting off from time to time into the clear sky. You are like Mary Magdalene, catching a glimpse of the Prince of Peace disguised as a gardener, or like the visitor to the Zen temple who discovers that the person cleaning the kitchen is the abbot. You become an explorer of the sacred ordinary, a connoisseur of the holy mess, a devotee of what is.

Awkward Metamorphosis

I was heartened when I heard that a butterfly is clumsy and disoriented when it first emerges from the cocoon. And that even when it does take flight, it can't seem to find a place to land. It alights on this flower and that one, chooses a twig and spends a few seconds there, still fluttering its wings, before rising into the sky again in search of a place to rest. That's how I feel much of the time. I think I'm growing, transforming, and that soon I'll have all my shit together and can burst forth from my latest metamorphosis ready to get on with the business of flying. Instead, I stumble around wondering what these strange objects are clinging to my shoulder blades. As it turns out, flying isn't all it was cracked up to be. It's exhausting.

Much as I'd like to think I've dismantled false structures of ultimate enlightenment, the shadow of the patriarchy lingers. I keep hoping I will finally get it right and become the ideal specimen of a spiritually awakened human, calm and kind, both self-actualized and selfless. But the only flawless butterfly is a dead butterfly, pinned and mounted. I choose life. An ever-unfolding adventure, involving multiple meltdowns and glorious reshapings.

Living as a mystic does not mean you conform to a preconceived notion of purity and perfection. You abide in your humanity. You are still going to make bad choices sometimes, lose your temper with people you love, engage in addictive behaviors, get caught in painful thought patterns you believe you should be free of, collapse into apathy in the face of catastrophic world events. What it does mean is that you can bear witness to your own experience of the human condition with curiosity and tenderness, recognizing that you are an integral member of the vast family of created beings and that this life is a school for waking up and growing closer to the divine, however you experience it.

The science of metamorphosis is a vibrant model for our ongoing transformations. Teresa of Avila recognized this in the sixteenth century. "You must have heard about the incredible way that silk comes into being," she writes in her mystical masterwork, *The Interior Castle*. "What a marvelous example of his wonders in creation! Only God could have invented something like this."[1] She goes on to describe in vivid detail the transformation of the "homely white worm" into a magnificent butterfly.

Modern entomology tells us that the driving motivation of the adult female butterfly is to find the perfect place to lay her eggs. She selects a plant she knows will become the first food for the newly hatched caterpillar. This is you. Your dreams—for yourself and the world—are precious eggs, and you seek out welcoming, nurturing spaces to deposit them. These gardens will be a

---

1 Teresa of Avila, *The Interior Castle*, trans. M. Starr (New York: Riverhead, 2002), 126.

continued source of nourishment as your tender visions transform into living realities.

When the caterpillar hatches, its job is to eat. And eat and eat. During its brief life, the caterpillar may grow to one hundred times its original size. To do all this growing, it must shed its skin again and again. And so it is with you. Sometimes recklessly, other times with discernment, you consume dharma (spiritual studies and practices), drawing sustenance from many sources. You eat teachings and teachers, psychotherapy and fitness, the neuroscience of trauma and mindfulness practice. You metabolize failures and violations, enlarge your capacity for integrating grief and loss. You subsist on awe and wonder, grow plump on gratitude.

The most enchanting, disconcerting, and inevitable stage of the process is when the caterpillar becomes a chrysalis. Once the caterpillar (or the silkworm!) is fully grown, it stops eating and suspends itself from a branch. It spins a silken cocoon and nestles itself inside. This is where the magic unfolds. Everything the caterpillar was begins to dissolve. It turns into a puddle of organic goop. Special cells that were present in the larva begin to rapidly multiply, providing energy for the emergence of an entirely new being. At first, these "imaginal" cells—the seeds of a future flying creature—operate independently. What remains of the caterpillar will perceive them as a threat and try to attack them. But they gather and connect with each other and begin to resonate at the same frequency, passing information back and forth between them, until they reach a tipping point.

Now things get even more interesting. These collections of imaginal cells expand their "awareness" and start tuning to the frequency of the butterflies that have come before them, drawing resonance from their discarded bodies. Energized by their fore-bears, they begin acting not as individual cells but as a multicell organism, and a butterfly is born.

Can you identify with this stage of metamorphosis? In times of great change, humans often respond by turning inward and rest-ing in the dark. If you stay present with the discomfort and do not turn away from unknowing, you begin to come undone. Crusty old ego structures soften and begin to dissolve. "I am a heterosexual, college-educated, single mother with a sarcastic sense of humor." *Going, going* . . . Cherished beliefs lose their grip on you, and you are released into the mystery. "I accept Jesus as the way, the truth, and the light and I also consider reincarnation a plausible possi-bility and I subscribe to the law of manifestation, so I try to think positive." *Gone.* You know nothing. You are nothing. And this feels exactly right.

There is a deeper knowing inside this deconstruction. It draws you to connect with community, to find your people and lift them up. To ask for help and receive it humbly. It compels you to listen for the wisdom of the ancestors whispering through your genetic heritage and your spiritual lineages. The ones who have come be-fore you are singing you into wholeness.

Once the imaginal cells have done their work, forming eyes and wings, genitals and antennae, the butterfly is ready to emerge. It wriggles its way out of the cocoon and into the world. But it is not quite ready to fly. Its wings are folded and crinkled. It stumbles, clinging to the remnants of its old cocoon with a couple of legs, reaching for the branch with two more, and letting the other two wave in the air. Gradually, it pumps its wings and charges them with butterfly blood. At last, plumped up and strong, it lifts off.

Where the caterpillar's task was to eat, the butterfly's joy is to reproduce. It flies off in search of a mate, and once it has found that mate and they have made their butterfly love, pressing their abdomens together in flight, the female butterfly finds the right plant on which to lay her eggs, and the cycle begins again.

Maybe it's like that for you, too. As you emerge from the cocoon of each new transformation, you need a minute. You have to stretch and wiggle, flex and turn. You look around, you listen, you check atmospheric conditions. Even then, your first attempts at flying are likely to be bumpy. You might flutter back to your old branch, try to take shelter in the carcass of your former cocoon, but you cannot find purchase there.

Teresa of Avila had a solution for this. Let go. Die to the old so that you can be reborn into something new. "We have learned exactly what to do," she reminds us. "Let's do it! Let it die. Let the silkworm die. This is the natural outcome once it has done what it was created to do. Then we will see God and see ourselves nestled inside his greatness like the silkworm in her cocoon."[2] This is what the mystics of all traditions mean when they urge us to "die before we die."

You do not have to believe in God to harness the power of annihilation and transformation. The process is written into the architecture of your soul. An excruciating breakup can be a chrysalis in

2 Teresa of Avila, *The Interior Castle*, trans. M. Starr (New York: Riverhead, 2002), 129.

which you dissolve and, guided by your own birthright of imaginal cells, become something new. When your last child moves out of the house, you are handed another invitation to die to an old way of being. The inspiration for any new work of art, or raised bed garden, or act of social justice, means co-creating a conducive environment for laying your eggs, knowing in your bones that any kind of fertilization will require some kind of death.

Teresa of Avila tells us that the butterfly can be restless. Once it has learned to fly, it might not feel like there is any place to land and catch its breath. Maybe this restlessness is not a problem to be solved but rather, an integral part of the ever-unfolding process of becoming. You plant new seeds. Some wither in the ground; others burst into bloom. You begin to come to peace with the ambiguity of it all. Instead of viewing the endlessly unfinished project of self-improvement as a malady to be cured, you embrace it as a condition of embodied existence. You do the best you can with the imperfect butterfly you are and give yourself to service. It's the only thing that makes sense.

You're Not in Trouble

Gazing through the eyes of love is the mystic's favorite occupation. But it is not only an outward-turning gaze. Shine those love-beams on your own dear self. If to be a mystic is to experience communion with all that is and to know it as fundamentally blessed, then you are not separate from that reality. You are as lovable as the ocean, the crying child, the serene yogi.

My brother-in-law, Lance, has a saying: *You're not in trouble.*

If you're anything like the rest of us, this message comes in handy at least a dozen times a day. I have totally adopted it. Sometimes I catch myself swirling in free-floating anxiety and I tune in. I recognize that it's connected to some vague sense that I've done something bad or wrong, and when I inquire further into that feeling, it leads me to a more fundamental belief that I *am* something bad or wrong. The former is rarely the case and the latter, well, never is. I am okay, just as I am. And so are you. The reason I can recognize that shame game is because it has such a familiar face. But I can tell you, it is a mask, my friend. And I've unveiled it enough to know that it covers something authentic and tender, something beautiful.

Next time you send an email and then second-guess yourself—*Did I sound needy or mean?*—peel back the covering and reveal your true face. If you're visiting your mother and your brother jumps up to do the dishes while you're still enjoying a glass of wine and you feel compelled to help, take a breath. See what happens if you defy the family culture for a minute. Maybe you will give other members an opportunity to deconstruct the familiar patterns of guilt and try something different, something imbued with a bit more self-love, like lingering at the table to tell another story, hear a new joke, miss someone who is missing. So, you threw a plastic container into the regular garbage instead of the recycling? The environmental catastrophe police are not going to go after you. You are not in trouble.

We are so hard on ourselves. We can't understand how it is that years of psychotherapy and silent retreats haven't neutralized all our neurotic tendencies. It can be such a relief to let go of the unhelpful (and untrue) notion that you should be cured by now of the personality quirks and mental patterns that have always plagued you. I'm sure you've made progress, and you will continue to grow. You will also fall right back into those old currents and flow downstream into the quagmire. What were you expecting? That you would become the wise guru meditating on the mountaintop? The radiant divine mother beaming her light upon all the pilgrims who make their way to sit at her holy feet? That some singular awakening is right around the corner, and pretty soon you will no longer be subject to the blunders and breakdowns from which the rest of us suffer?

Good luck trying to recover from the human condition.

I once heard a description of a condition Buddhists call *dukkha dukkha*. The Pali word *dukkha* is often translated as "pain." When we have a direct experience of pain and stay present to it, we can breathe a big enough space around the feeling to contain it. A toothache, for instance, or a surge of jealousy, or a rotator cuff injury, or a fight with your best friend. But most of us tell ourselves a story about the experience: *This totally sucks; I'm probably going to need shoulder surgery.* Or, *I guess that relationship is over; she'll never speak to me again after I pointed out that thing she did eleven years ago that I never mentioned till now when I needed ammunition.* That's when we add *dukkha* to *dukkha*. Double *dukkha* equals suffering.

Can you please be kind to yourself, even if just for a minute? Can you forgive your real transgressions, make amends, and move on with humility and humor? Can you stop inventing fake transgressions and carrying them like wounds in the palms of your hands, rubbing them until they become infected? Even Gandhi was impatient with his wife and the Dalai Lama implied that homo-sexuality is unnatural. Yes, certain female spiritual icons have been known to use Botox. The enlightenment journey is just that: a journey. We unfold and grow as we go. Anyone who pretends that they are finished is lying to themselves and bamboozling you. Give your sweet self a break for being a regular person on a path of awakening. You are not in trouble.

Bodhisattvas in Disguise

I confess: I like to have my nails done. Even as a hippie girl in col-lege when I rarely wore a bra and wasn't exactly sure how to apply mascara, I painted my nails. They looked like jewels on the ends of my fingers and made me smile. I have carried this guilty pleasure all through adulthood. My local nail salon is a temple, and Michelle is the high priestess who presides there.

At first, I did not recognize Michelle for the bodhisattva she is. Like most mystics, she was in disguise. A young beauty from Vietnam, Michelle wore tight polyester pants, shimmery tops, and high-heeled sandals in the middle of winter. She did not make eye contact; rarely spoke, even in response to something I said; and seemed vaguely annoyed by my presence. But she wasn't. She just didn't waste time on the superficial American custom of small talk. Rather than taking it personally, I opted to join Michelle in her si-lence. And little by little, over months and years, we entered into a kind of sacred communion. Her family grew, her business flour-ished, and I bore witness. We both started working out at the same gym, lifting weights side by side.

One day, as my nails were drying under the UV light, Michelle made an offhand comment about the time she was in a refugee camp in Hong Kong. My ears perked up. I asked a question. She answered me, chuckling as she recalled leaving her village in Vietnam at the age of fourteen without shoes on her feet, and how cold it was on the boat. After a few more sessions at the salon, I asked another question. She told me that fifty people were crammed into a canoe meant for a dozen, and that they were starving. Mere meters from the shore, the boat capsized, and many passengers drowned. Michelle, who did not know how to swim, clung to the vessel for hours before the boat was righted and, leaving the dead behind, they continued their journey. Michelle's parents were informed that their teenaged daughter was among the deceased, and it was months before she was able to make contact and assure them that she had survived. To escape detection, the refugees rowed at night, hugging the shore.

When they reached Hong Kong, the camps were overflowing. Gangs ruled. Young girls like Michelle were not safe to walk alone. Residents were forbidden to leave the fenced compound. They were dependent on the Chinese government to meet their most basic needs for shelter, clothing, and food, all of which were inadequate. The camps functioned more as detention centers than as places of refuge.

Over time, as Michelle's story unfolded, told in her quiet voice behind the folds of her paper mask, I remembered that we can never know what another person has been through, what drives their behavior or motivates their actions. The car that zips around yours and then weaves in and out of traffic to get ahead may be carrying a woman in labor. The clerk at the department of motor vehicles who brusquely sends you away on account of what seems to you like an insignificant lack of documentation may be grieving the recent death of her daughter from leukemia. The aloof nail technician may have barely survived a harrowing boat trip on the South China Sea, followed by five years in a refugee camp.

The more I opened my heart to Michelle, the more of her own heart she revealed. Last winter was especially cold in our mountain town. Our unhoused neighbors were suffering. One night, there was a break-in at Michelle's salon. When the police apprehended the perpetrator, a man who was camped with his dog in the back of a crumbling parking lot nearby, she refused to press charges. She did not demand her money back. "He obviously needs it more than we do," she told me. This, coming from a woman who started off with nothing, who, along with her husband, Henry, worked seven days a week so that their children could go to college. When she returns to Vietnam to visit, she takes suitcases stuffed with electronic gadgets and chocolates for her family, and wads of one-dollar bills to give out to the beggars who line up at her parents' door the moment word gets out that relatives have arrived from the United States.

"How did you get this way?" I ask Michelle, expecting her to say that the hardship she has endured awakened her compassion for others.

"Thich Nhat Hanh," she tells me.

"The Zen monk?"

"Yes, I listen to his talks on YouTube."

Like Michelle, Thich Nhat Hanh was from Vietnam, though she

knew nothing about him until she had lived in the United States for decades and assimilated into the culture. But her bodhisattva heart resonated with his. The gentle monk taught that love is intertwined with understanding, and that to develop understanding you have to practice looking at all beings through the eyes of compassion. Then, you cannot help but love them, and you naturally do whatever is in your power to alleviate their suffering. This teaching has shaped Michelle's philosophy of life.

To be an ordinary mystic is to lead with love, to prioritize compassion, to regard the world with a sincere desire to see the goodness in others. When we are on the lookout for unity, we see it everywhere. And we embody it. Don't go searching for the masters of the mystical gaze standing at the pulpits and teaching in the yoga studios. Or at least not exclusively. The true sages may be hiding in plain sight in the toothless woman at an all-night convenience store in the sketchiest neighborhood of your city, in the veterinarian who puts your dog to sleep, in the child selling mangos on a stick on your vacation to Mazatlán.

Decolonize Spirituality

The fastest growing religious category in the United States is not Zen Buddhism. It's not Zoroastrianism or Pentecostalism. It isn't even atheism. It's the Nones, that is, those who check the "None" box on questionnaires about religious affiliation, those who consider themselves to be "spiritual but not religious." These are people who may not subscribe to a set of religious propositions, engage in traditional spiritual practices, or attend church. But they are often people whose hearts are open, who seek wisdom, who believe in treating all beings and the earth with reverence. Does this sound like you?

I think of permaculture, where cucumbers intertwine with morning glory vines, where berry patches thrive alongside winter wheat, where rainwater is collected and channeled as needed and herbs grow right outside the kitchen door for easy access. There is an untamed and untamable quality at the heart of permaculture, and also a consciously cultivated relationship with the earth, rooted in deep listening and a holistic systems perspective in which everything is connected with and responsive to everything else. And then I think of a proper suburban garden, with neatly tended hedges and flowers planted as if painted by numbers. There is little room for deviation or innovation in a formal garden. Wildness is controlled. The ordinary mystic flourishes in an ecosystem of spiritual diversity.

The Spiritual Boys' Club is fond of recommending that, instead of harvesting a little mindfulness practice here, some Gospel of John there, and a sprig of Sufi poetry over yonder, you "pick one path" (preferably whichever tradition happens to be theirs) and "go deep." The implication is that otherwise you would be just skimming the surface and missing out on the real nourishment that comes with committing to the rigors of a singular faith. They decry an interspiritual approach as "New Age." I don't know about you, but I find the term New Age insulting. It evokes middle-aged white women in flowing garments—some goofy admixture of Indian and Celtic—reading each other's auras and washing their crystals in moonlight. Are these our only choices? Episcopalian or fake-pagan?

A rapidly growing population of American seekers are rooting themselves in the generous and creative space of spiritual but not religious. They believe in a reality that simultaneously transcends and encompasses our everyday experience. They may resist calling it God, but they have no trouble naming it as Love. They are dedicated to awakening this force in their own lives and sharing it in community. They are finding each other, gathering in small groups that are less inclined to proclaim some credo than to affirm the truth of interbeing. They value art and literature, they uphold the separation of church and state yet refuse to separate politics from the life of the soul, and they offer the fruits of their practices to the well-being of the world. This is the path of ordinary mysticism. It is both private and communal. It is embodied and transcendent. It is regular and brimming with light.

This does not mean that the people who are devoted to a religion are caught in the past and incapable of living mystical moments. There is great value in investing in the disciplines of prayer and meditation, in knowing the scriptures and history of your faith. I often wish I were more fluent in Hindu mythology or Kabbalah so that I could claim adequate credibility when I use an example from the *Mahabharata* or refer to the Tree of Life in my teachings and writings. But I have been unwilling to sacrifice the wildness for authority. I refuse to forsake the mystery for the sake of consistency. I cannot bring myself to confine my intimacy with the sacred within the halls of a religious institution. Does this resonate with you? If so, you are not alone. Our numbers are burgeoning.

The trick is not to treat spiritual resources from other cultures as nothing more than another commodity to consume. Rather, when you are practicing yoga in your local studio, educate yourself about the landscape from which these practices grew, the language that names them, the deities that shape them. Whether you are sharing what you've heard about Iroquois philosophy at a Thanksgiving dinner or tattooing an Arabic phrase on your forearm, pay homage to the source. Capitalism has the nasty habit of exploiting the marginalized for the sake of accumulating more. More wealth, more power, more status and control. Don't fall for it. Wisdom is not a thing to acquire. Love is far wilder than commerce, and more interesting. Decolonize spirituality.

Cradled in the Well of My Body

When my friend Sará was in tenth grade, her family moved from rural Minnesota to Compton, California. It was the early 2000s, not long after the Columbine shooting, when the virus of gun violence was beginning to show signs of becoming a pandemic. Suddenly, Sará was surrounded by gun violence in her new town. She was lucky, however, because she had access to a good education that kept her outside of the circles of conflict that impacted her peers. She was accepted into a medical magnate school, where high school students got to spend a day each week shadowing a doctor at the hospital across the street or working with research scientists in the lab. When it came time to choose their assignment, Sará volunteered to work in the morgue.

The morgue? What fifteen-year-old would willingly choose to spend hours in the company of the dead?

"I thought I was being all goth," Sará admits. But there was a deeper impulse, beyond teenage edginess. "Something in me wanted to pull back the veil on death. It was around me all the time anyway, just going to school, walking through the neighborhood, eating my lunch."

One day, the lab tech went on an errand, and Sará, alone in the morgue, became curious about one particular drawer, and she opened it. She was shocked to see a boy her own age, with skin the color of hers, lying on the cold steel slab. "He was perfect in every way," Sará tells me. "He had this big, gorgeous, ebullient afro and the cutest clothes. I was confused. I thought one of my classmates was playing a prank on me."

Transfixed, Sará crouched over the drawer and gazed at the beautiful boy. That's when she noticed a tiny hole in the center of his forehead. "It was like a bomb went off inside me. My body flew back with the realization of how he had died." She gingerly closed the drawer and sat in stunned stillness, contemplating the mirror of the dead boy's face, wondering whether this could happen to her.

When the lab tech returned, Sará confessed what she had done, and asked whether he knew how this boy had come to be there. He told her that a couple of days before, the boy had been walking home from school and got caught in the crossfire of two rival gangs.

"I have walked with the memory of this young man's face ever since," Sará tells me. "His hair and his clothes. His heart; his being. He was one of my first teachers." She describes the immediate kinship she felt with him and the stark contrast that he was no longer living while she carried this life force, this breath still animating her body.

"The gong of all gongs went off that day," Sará says. Without words, she knew she was being handed a mission of some sort. "What could someone like me possibly do in response to a situation like this?" She was determined to figure it out.

Sará began a journey of investigating the roots of gun violence, exploring its impact not only on communities of color in the United States, but on the whole of the human family, and the earth itself. She pulled on one thread and discovered it was linked to an entire tapestry of suffering. Question upon question arose. How was gun violence related to the prison industrial complex, to war, to slavery, to capitalism, patriarchy, imperialism, colonialism? This process of fearless inquiry was not liberating, however. It was soul-crushing. Desperate to connect to a source of aliveness deeper than anything she could access with her scientific mind, Sará turned to yoga and meditation.

"I came to cradle the suffering in the well of my body," she says.

This is the path of the ordinary mystic, expanding our hearts to contain the pain of the world and transmute it with love. Not transcend it, but tenderly integrate suffering into the vastness of who we are. "The sacred and the mystical are key to our ability to return to our aliveness," Sará tells me. "They open us to the awe and wonder of knowing ourselves as descended from stars." Sará reminds me that this "gorgeous well of resourcefulness" is available to all of us when we dare to resist society's pressure to do more, do it faster, keep up. The invitation is to slow down enough to detect the miracle of aliveness welling out of everything within and around us. This effulgence is intimately entwined with emptiness. Contemplative practices help us to rest in the dynamic abundance found in deep stillness.

Sará is now a neuroscientist, working at the edges of the mystery. "I walk hand in hand with my bestie, paradox," Sará says. "We roll deep, they and I."

Mystics have always known that reality is a dance of opposites. It is in the quiet that we find the music; in solitude, true community. By following the threads of injustice, we arrive at foundational goodness. In opening ourselves to the depths of suffering, we are blessed with the capacity to cradle the heart of the world.

Darkness, Light

Sometimes the sacred breaks through the cracks in our lives and lights up everything. A beloved dog is hit by a car and dies in your arms by the side of the road. She gazes at you with unconditional trust as her heart slows to a stop. Sometimes we are gifted with moments of perfect peace. Your children and their children come for a visit and you watch them messing around in the kitchen as they fry tortillas and grate cheese, cracking each other up, and you would not exchange this moment for anything. Something in you knows that the next catastrophe is even now preparing to break across the horizon: adultery or disease, money troubles or an addicted teenager. Experiences of both affliction and epiphany are woven into the human condition, and the ordinary mystic does not push either away.

You have countless opportunities to grow through life's

challenges—in other words, to become an ever more fully, deeply *human* human being. This is the meaning of the Yiddish word *mensch*. Someone whose humanity shines through the darkness of this world. Someone who believes in the fundamental goodness of life and embodies it. Not despite challenging experiences, but as the result of having practiced facing them with courage and kindness.

In the Hindu pantheon, Brahma creates the universe, Vishnu sustains it, and Shiva destroys it. Shiva is the god of transformation. But his power to make all things new lies in his power to destroy the old. When I was a teenager, Ram Dass, who spent a lot of time in India, told me that this world is Shiva's dream. Shiva is asleep on Mount Kailash, and when he wakes up, Ram Dass said, he will dance in a circle of fire, and then illusion will fall away and we will all be liberated. Now that I am in my sixties and have suffered shattering losses (including the loss of Ram Dass) and endured unbidden transformations, I recognize the footprints of the dancing Shiva all over the landscape of my life.

The invitation is to embrace the many crucifixions this life presents and say yes to the ongoing resurrections that unfold. Die to the old to rebirth the new. Again and again. Your story is not finished.

Practice

DAY OF SILENCE

Choose a day to not speak, from the time you wake in the morning through going to sleep at night. Tell the people in your life that you are going to be doing this so that they will not be concerned for your mental health. You can use pen and paper (or electronic devices) to write notes but should keep even this form of verbal communication to a minimum. See if you can silence your environment, too. Turn off the TV, don't slip those electronic buds into your ears, and avoid crowded spaces filled with human chatter, like gyms and bars.

When you are finished, journal about your experience, or tell someone you trust what it was like for you, what you discovered in the well of quiet.

⋉

WRITING PROMPT

I never would have believed . . .

Epilogue

Standing on Holy Ground

Take Off Your Sandals

Walk with me through a little midrash, an imaginative exploration of a familiar story from the Hebrew scriptures. Indulge me as I change the gender of the protagonist.

Moses is herding her flock on Mount Horeb in Egypt when she hears the crackling sound of fire. Uh-oh. Danger! She looks around for the source of the blaze, ready to smother it with her cloak and douse it with her flagon of water. She spies a bramble bush engulfed in flame, but its leaves seem to be untouched. The bush is burning, but it is not burning up. Then she hears a voice call her name.

"Moses!"

She looks around, bewildered. And the voice calls again.

"Moses!"

The voice is emanating from within the fiery foliage.

"Take off your sandals, Moses," the voice demands. "You are standing on holy ground."

Moses unties her laces and slips off her shoes. She unfolds her body on the desert floor and presses her face into the dust. This is the moment when Moses meets her life. She meets it empty and in silence. She was not prepared for this encounter, yet everything that came before readied her for it.

Many years ago, when Moses was a baby, a terrible Egyptian pharaoh decreed that all Israelites be killed at birth. At the same time as the midwives delivered them to life, they were ordered to send them to their deaths. Moses's mother, Yocheved, and Moses's older sister, Miriam, hatched a desperate plot to save her. They wove a basket of papyrus, coated it with sap, placed the baby in it, and sent it down the Nile River, hoping someone would find the floating cradle and save the infant Moses. Miriam ran along the shore, hiding in the bulrushes, until her baby sister washed up on the riverbank where Pharaoh's daughter was bathing with friends. Captivated, the young princess took the baby home and asked her parents if they could keep her, raising her in the royal household as one of their own.

Miriam ran back to fetch her mother. They knocked on the palace gates.

"We heard you adopted an orphaned child," Miriam told Pharaoh. "As it happens, this woman's baby just died." The fact that the man who stood in the doorway with his wife and his daughter, who held the infant Moses in her arms, was likely responsible for the death of the woman's baby remained unspoken, hanging in the air between them like a thundercloud. "You will be needing a wet nurse, and she has milk."

And so, unknowingly, Pharaoh hired Moses's own mother to nurse her.

The Israelite Moses grew up thinking she was Egyptian. When she was a teenager, she witnessed a slave driver savagely abusing an Israelite slave, and she lost it. She grabbed a nearby stone and hurled it at the guy's head, killing him. Knowing her foster father would punish her, possibly even have her executed for treason, she fled into the mountains, fending for herself, finally settling in a small Midianite village and marrying one of the seven sons of the village shaman, Jethro. They had two children together, and Moses settled serenely into life as a simple shepherd.

The Egyptian pharaohs had not always been despots. Back in Jacob and Joseph's day, the pharaoh was neighborly. When famine in Canaan drove Jacob's family to seek refuge with his long-lost son Joseph in Egypt, the pharaoh took them in, and they ended up staying. The Israelite community flourished in Egypt. But they became too prosperous for the new generations of Egyptian rulers, who perceived them as a threat and enslaved them as a labor force to build the pyramids. It was this unjust dynamic that caused young Moses to snap.

Which brings Moses to this moment, body spread like honey on the bread of the desert, the voice of the Holy One calling her name.

"Who are you?" she asks.

"I am the God of your ancestors," the voice answers. "I have witnessed the suffering of your people and now I am going to liberate them. I have chosen you to be my mouthpiece. You are going to go back to Egypt and demand that Pharaoh set them free."

This made Moses sit up and speak directly into the bush that was burning but not being consumed.

"Me?" She almost laughed. "I am nobody! A poor shepherd. Besides, Pharaoh wanted to kill me, remember? Plus, I stutter."

"Who do you think made your mouth?" the Holy One pointed out. "I will be with you."

"I can't," Moses pleaded. "Please don't make me."

"Okay, tell you what," said the God of her ancestors. "I'll appoint your brother, Aaron, to speak for you. I communicate with you, you pass it along to him, and he conveys the message to the Egyptians. And your sister, Miriam, will lead the way, singing and dancing."

This was a watershed moment, and Moses knew it. There was no turning back to the life she had known, herding her father-in-law's flock, cooking for her family on a stone hearth, singing the old songs her mother-in-law taught her. There was only a flowing forward, into the unknown.

"*Hineyni*," Moses said, as Mother Mary would say thousands of years later, as the Prophet Muhammad would say, and as Nelson Mandela and Greta Thunberg would one day say. "Here I am."

What are your watershed moments?—those times when you are minding your own business, doing your thing, and the sacred breaks through some regular activity and changes everything. Maybe you've popped into the supermarket for pasta on your way home from work and your eye catches the eye of a little boy, his legs dangling from his mother's cart, and he holds your gaze. In his face you see innocence and wonder, and you also glimpse a flash of his life ahead, filled with both magic and disillusionment, with loss and with grace, and your own eyes grow damp with an almost unbearable wave of love. In him, you see yourself; and in yourself, all beings. You will never recover from this. You would not want to.

This is what it means to be an ordinary mystic. Don't you realize that you are one? That your fleeting tastes of unitive awareness qualify as mystical? That when unconditional mercy washes over you, the divine is remaking your heart? Your only possible response in these moments is to take off your shoes and press yourself to the ground. To grow quiet enough to hear the wings of the angels beating the air around you, still enough to allow yourself to be transfigured. And then, get up and get to work. The liberation of all beings is tied up with your own awakening.

Barefoot

In the sixteenth century, Teresa of Avila risked everything to reform the Carmelite Order. She had to push up against the power structure of a church she loved, defy the Spanish Inquisition, and endure relentless persecution. What was the message she dared to proclaim, the values she sought to reclaim, the source of such disdain?

Simplify.

Return to your contemplative roots. Be like the desert mothers and fathers who sought God in silence and solitude, and, recognizing the essential unity of all that is, turned back outward to serve community. Turning and returning. In Hebrew, the word is *teshuvah*. Stripping ourselves of distraction, through prayer and service, we continually, ongoingly, wholeheartedly realign ourselves with the divine.

In honor of this commitment to voluntary simplicity, Teresa called her reform movement the Discalced Carmelites, that is, the "barefoot" Carmelites. Like Moses, whose only possible response to the holy presence was to remove her shoes, Teresa's companions recognized that the mystical life requires radical nakedness. The intimacy our souls long for can happen only when we take off whatever stands between ourselves and union with the One. Our hunger for new cars and clothes, our reliance on other people's opinions of us, our preconceptions about what it means to be spiritual, our attachment to habitual states of misery. Take it off. Peel it off and fling it off. Find your own subversive spirit and reclaim even the most challenging parts of your life as holy ground. Then everyday miracles will spring from beneath your bare feet to astonish you.

Rain of Yes

All my life, I have been enamored of the God-intoxicated ones. Those rarified souls who slip into ecstatic states and spontaneously utter poetry. The ones who exude deep stillness, embody equanimity, listen more than they speak. The initiated and the ordained, the monastics. You could recognize them by their white robes or their headscarves, the prayer beads wound around their wrists and the scriptures from which they quote. If a talk show host wanted to interview a mystic, these are the exemplars they would invite into the studio.

I wanted to be one of them.

Until I didn't.

I want you not to want that as well. Instead, I want you to want exactly what you have: a real life, with its clogged plumbing and flight delays, its cool sheets and steaming showers, its free-floating anxieties and spontaneous foot rubs. Girl's Night Out, Monday Night Football, the death of your favorite uncle and the birth of your first grandchild. Comings out and turnings in. Your crises of faith. I want you to want to be exactly who you are: a true human person doing their best to show up for this fleeting life with a measure of grace, with kindness and a sense of humor, with curiosity and a willingness to not have all the answers, with reverence for life.

You do not need to chant all night in a temple in the Himalayas. You don't have to be the newest incarnation of Mary Magdalene. It is not necessary to read or write spiritual books. You are not required to know the difference between Mahayana and Theravada Buddhism or memorize the Beatitudes. All you have to do to walk the path of the ordinary mystic is to cultivate a gaze of wonder and step onto the road. Keep walking. Rest up, and walk again. Fall down, get up, walk on. Pay attention to the landscape. To the ways it changes and the ways it stays the same. Be alert to surprises and turn with the turning of the seasons. Honor your body, train your mind, and keep your heart open against all odds. Say yes to what is, even when it is uncomfortable or embarrassing or heartbreaking. Hurl your handful of yes into the treetops and then lift your face as the rain of yes drops its grace all over you, all around you, and settles deep inside you.

ACKNOWLEDGMENTS

Deepest gratitude to all the ordinary mystics who light up my life and inspired this book, especially:

Susanna Starr, Amy Starr, Roy Starr, Kali Little Martinez, Daniela Whitehorse, Jenny Bird, Nancy Laupheimer, Tot Tatarsky, Willow Brook, Kelly Notaras, Andrew Harvey, Bill McNichols, Anil Molares Singh, Greta Roningen, Richard Rohr, Annie Lamott, Nina Rao, Caroline Myss, Tirzah Firestone, Natalie Goldberg, James Finley, Greg Boyle, Matthew Fox. And to all my little grandpeople: Jacob, Bree, Metztli, Niko, Sol, Naya, Aaliyah, and Malika, who already make this world make more sense.

Special gratitude to the light of my life, Ganga Das Jeff Little, the embodiment of everyday wisdom and my constant refuge.

I always work best when I can get away for a few days at a time to drop all the way in. To the people who offered me beautiful places to write in solitude and silence: Amanda Dean, Kelly Notaras, Andy and Ruthelen Burns. Early in the process of working on this book, Jeff and I made an offer on a beautiful property bordering the national forest where we hike every day and then had to withdraw when we realized we really couldn't afford it. One of the best features was a private studio where I could write. A few months later, I crossed paths with a woman I had never seen before on that trail. "Are you Mirabai Starr?" she asked. "I am," I admitted. She said she loved my books and had heard I lived somewhere nearby and had hoped to run into me one day. I asked where she lived, and she told me she had recently bought the very house we had tried to buy. She had no idea we were the ones who made it possible for her to become a steward of the land she loved, and we both marveled as it all came into focus. They were using it as a vacation rental for now, hoping one day to move in full time. "You know, Mirabai, you can write there when we don't have bookings," she said. And so it is that I have written much of this book in that very house. So, thank you to Chelona and Nelson Zink, and to Katie Raver. What a miracle.

When my beloved longtime agent, Sarah Jane Freymann, retired a couple of years ago, I despaired of ever finding anyone who would "get me" like she did, who would champion me and feed me and draw out the best in me. I was wrong. Finding Amanda Annis (thank you, *querida* Ana Ban, for matchmaking us!) has been a great boon. She shares my sweet spot: a passion for the confluence of the literary and the spiritual. I am grateful for you, Amanda. Being paired with Anna Paustenbach and her team at HarperOne is another beautiful fit for which I am deeply grateful. Anna's steady care, wise insight, and kind regard have contributed greatly to the joyous flow of these pages. I will always be grateful to Tami Simon and the Sounds True family for publishing so many of my previous books. Your love and support run like a ribbon of light through everything else I write.

The most profound gratitude of all goes to Annie Lamott, who planted the seed for this book, encouraged me to write it, and watered the garden all along.

ABOUT THE AUTHOR

Mirabai Starr is an award-winning author, internationally acclaimed speaker, and a leading teacher of interspiritual dialogue. In 2020, she was honored on *Watkins*'s list of the 100 Most Spiritually Influential Living People. Drawing from twenty years of teaching philosophy and world religions at the University of New Mexico—Taos, Mirabai now travels the world sharing her wisdom on contemplative living, writing as a spiritual practice, and the transformational power of grief and loss. She has authored over a dozen books including *Wild Mercy*, *Caravan of No Despair*, and *God of Love: A Guide to the Heart of Judaism, Christianity and Islam*. Mirabai has received critical acclaim for her revolutionary contemporary translations of the mystics John of the Cross, Teresa of Avila, and Julian of Norwich. Mirabai offers the fruit of decades of study, teaching, and contemplative practice in a fresh, grounded, and lyrical voice to a growing circle of folks inspired by the life-giving essence of feminine wisdom. Mirabai continues to teach seminars, workshops, and retreats, both in person and through her online community Wild Heart. She lives with her extended family in the mountains of northern New Mexico. For more, visit www.mirabaistarr.com.